Authors in Their Age

JANE AUSTEN

Valerie Grosvenor Myer

BLACKIE

BLACKIE & SON LIMITED
Bishopbriggs Glasgow G64 2NZ
Furnival House 14–18 High Holborn London WC1V 6BX

For Lois Spencer, in gratitude

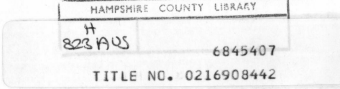
Cover portrait of Jane Austen by Cassandra Austen
reproduced by courtesy of the National Portrait Gallery, London

Printed in Great Britain by
Thomson Litho Ltd, East Kilbride, Scotland

Authors in Their Age

JANE AUSTEN

Authors in Their Age

Authors in Their Age is a series of introductions to the work of major authors in English literature. Each book provides the background information that can help a reader see such an author in context, involved in and reacting to the society of which he was a part.

Some volumes are devoted to individual authors such as Chaucer and Wordsworth. Others look at a particular period in our literary history in which an author can be seen as representative of his time—for example, *The Age of Keats and Shelley* and *The Age of Lawrence*.

There is no attempt to impose a standard format on each of the books. However, all the books provide biographical material and deal with the important political, social and cultural movements of the time. Each book considers the author's readership, the problems of editing his or her work and the major influences on his or her writing. All are well illustrated with drawings, documents or photographs of the time.

There is also a guide to further reading and other source material which will enable the student to progress to a more detailed study of the writer's work and its treatment by literary critics.

Anthony Adams
Esmor Jones
General Editors

Contents

I

Life and times

Jane Austen was born in 1775, the daughter of a country rector, the Rev. George Austen, and his wife Cassandra, whose grandmother had been sister to a Duke. Jane was the seventh of eight children; her only sister, Cassandra, two years older than herself, was her greatest friend. Their mother said that if Cassandra were going to have her head cut off, Jane would insist on having hers cut off too. Most of Jane's surviving letters were written to Cassandra. Unfortunately, after Jane died at the age of forty-two, Cassandra destroyed those letters she felt were too private for posterity.

Jane was considered attractive: slender, fairly tall, with a pleasant speaking voice. Neither sister married. Cassandra's fiancé, Thomas Fowle, died of yellow fever in the West Indies in 1796. Jane accepted a proposal of marriage from Harrison Bigg-Wither on 2nd December 1802, but, after sleeping on her decision, changed her mind.

Women of the upper middle class, to which they belonged, stayed at home till they married. Neither daughter ever left home. Jane Austen's days were spent helping to run the household, which had its own dairy, baked its own bread, brewed its own ale and held mammoth wash days (generally, at that time, once a month). Although Edward Austen-Leigh, in his memoir of his aunt, says that Jane and Cassandra did not do the actual work themselves, all this must have taken some organizing. Evenings were spent in music (Jane sang and played the piano, like other young ladies), sewing, visiting, receiving visits from neighbours and friends, card parties and balls. Jane was popular with her numerous nephews and nieces, always ready to amuse them. In later life, she gave them criticism and encouragement when they tried their hands at fiction.

In 1782 the girls were sent to school in Oxford, to a Mrs Cawley, a connection by marriage. After a year, Mrs Cawley, who seems to have been rather severe, moved to Southampton, and the girls moved with her. But their parents took them away

Portrait of Jane Austen engraved for the *Memoir* of his aunt by the Rev. J. Edward Austen-Leigh, published 1870 (The Fotomas Index)

when they caught '*putrid sore throat*' (probably diphtheria) and Jane nearly died.

A year or two later, they were sent to the Abbey School at Reading where they were happier. But they only stayed a few months. Jane's real education took place between the ages of nine and sixteen, when she had the run of her father's books. When she was twenty-one he treated her to a copy of Fanny Burney's novel, *Camilla*; Jane's name appears on the list of subscribers to the first edition.

Jane's brother Henry wrote after her death of their father:

> *Being not only a profound scholar but possessing a most exquisite taste in every species of literature, it is not*

*wonderful that his daughter Jane should at a very early age
have become sensible to the charms of style and enthusiastic
in the cultivation of her own language.*

In 1801 the family moved from Steventon, in Hampshire,
where Jane was born, to Bath, which she disliked. Four years
later, Mr Austen died. *'His tenderness as a father, who can do
justice to?'*, wrote Jane on 22nd January 1805 to her elder brother
Francis who was in the Navy, telling him the news. A year later,
the widow and daughters moved to Southampton. In 1809 they
moved back to Hampshire, to Chawton, near the second son,
Edward. Like characters in Jane Austen's novels (Frank
Churchill in *Emma*, Fanny Price in *Mansfield Park*), Edward had
been adopted when a child by a rich relative, Thomas Knight,
and had changed his name to Knight. This Thomas Knight was
the patron of a living: he had the power to appoint clergy to the
position of vicar (rector in some parishes) and had at one time
given a living to Jane Austen's father. Three of her novels hinge
on young clergymen having to wait for livings before they can
marry, until an influential patron can be found to give them one.
Edward was able to help his mother and sisters, who lived with
their friend, Martha Lloyd, with money and gifts of fruit and
game from his considerable estate.

Jane Austen's house at Chawton is now a museum. Visitors
can view the creaking door Jane left unoiled so she could get
warning if anybody approached while she was writing at her
desk. If the hinge squeaked, she would hide her manuscript
under other papers. She has left us six complete novels and
various fragments.

She started writing in her early teens, making up parodies and
plays to entertain her family. When she was fifteen, she wrote
*The History of England, by A Partial, Prejudiced and Ignorant
Historian,* adding, *'N.B. There will be very few dates in this
history.'.* The 'History' demonstrates her neat turn of phrase and
love of a joke, together with independent opinions: of Henry
VIII she writes that *'his only merit was his not being* quite *so bad
as his daughter Elizabeth'.*

Jane prefers Mary, Queen of Scots, who was *'constant in her
religion'.* Indeed, her principal reason for writing was *'to prove
the innocence of the Queen of Scotland'.* Jane also sympathized
with Charles I against the 'gang' of rebels. Her sympathies, all
her life, were Royalist and conservative, which creates difficulties

Queen Elizabeth I, drawn by Cassandra Austen for Jane's *The history of England by a partial, prejudiced and ignorant historian* which she wrote in 1791.

for some readers of her novels. She was fond of reading history. In the margin of her copy of Oliver Goldsmith's history of England, she wrote: '*Every ancient custom ought to be sacred, unless it is prejudicial to happiness.*'

Sense and Sensibility was published in 1811; *Pride and Prejudice* in 1813; *Mansfield Park* in 1814; *Emma* in 1816. *Northanger Abbey* (written first but not published, although accepted) was bought back by her brother Henry and published together with her last novel, *Persuasion*, in 1818, after her death.

She had a kidney complaint. Knowing she was seriously ill, she moved to 8 College Street, Winchester, for treatment by a Mr Lyford, but it was ineffective. During her last illness, it was her custom to lie on three chairs, so that her mother (who seems to have grown increasingly difficult and hypochondriacal) could have the sofa. Jane died in Cassandra's arms on 18th July 1817. She is buried in the North Aisle of Winchester Cathedral.

The world Jane Austen was born into was, in some respects, very different from our own. During the second half of the eighteenth century, the old cart tracks had been replaced to some extent by good roads, but all travel was limited to the speed of the horse. Many people lived and died in the villages where they had been born. But this pattern was changing, as enclosures of common land earlier in the century had made large-scale, more efficient farming possible. Smallholders and graziers, driven away by the great landowners, shifted to the manufacturing towns, to work in factories.

Yet this change, which was to be so important in transforming Britain, was not yet visible in the villages dominated by the squire, with his tenant farmers, and the parson. This is the '*confined and unvarying society*'[1] Jane Austen writes about. Many of her characters experience social friction, forced to move constantly among people they dislike, but cannot escape from.   In his *Enquiry Into the Duties of the Female Sex* (a book Jane Austen seems to have liked), published 1796, the Rev. Thomas Gisborne wrote:

To the daughter of a country gentleman, the paternal mansion, insulated in its park, or admitting no contiguous habitation except the neighbouring hamlet, seldom furnishes the opportunity of access to a perpetual circle of amusements. Visitors are not always to be found in the drawing room; the card-table cannot always be fitted up; the country town affords a ball but once a month.

This is the social world Jane Austen writes about, that inhabited by the daughters of country gentlemen. On 3rd January 1801, she wrote to Cassandra:

We have lived long enough in this neighbourhood, the Basingstoke balls are certainly on the decline, there is something interesting in the bustle of going away, and the prospect of spending future summers by the sea or in Wales is very delightful.

The Rev. Thomas Gisborne comments that however quiet the life of a gentleman's daughter might be, '*there is no place which affords an exemption from the obligation of rational pursuits and mental improvement*'. It is clear from her novels that Jane Austen accepted this view of life.

Her life, and the lives of her characters, strike us as tranquil to the point of monotony. Jane Austen never travelled abroad. Yet she lived through years of anxiety, upheaval, misery and bloodshed. Her brothers Francis (Frank) and Charles fought against Napoleon's Navy and both rose to be admirals. They corresponded with their sister from all over the world, and she took a keen interest in the progress of the war and in public events. She has been criticized for not reflecting, in her fiction, the violence of the times in which she lived, nor their more explicit political realities.

But even in wartime, the effect of the fighting on the lives of those at home is marginal, except when relatives are killed. Those left to keep things going are concerned with their homes, their families, their careers, social relationships, the books they read, the music they play or listen to, the pictures they see.

In November 1815, Mr J. S. Clarke, librarian to the Prince Regent, wrote inviting her to dedicate her next work to the Prince. Mr Clarke, a clergyman, also asked her to write about '*a clergyman, who should pass his time between the metropolis and the country*'.

Tactfully, Jane replied that she was honoured. Writing on 11th December 1815, she said:

> *The comic part of the character I might be equal to, but not the good, the enthusiastic, the literary. Such a man's conversation must at times be on subjects of science and philosophy, of which I know nothing; or at least be occasionally abundant in quotations and allusions which a woman who, like me, knows only her own mother tongue, and has read very little in that, would be totally without the power of giving. A classical education, or at any rate a very extensive acquaintance with English literature, ancient and modern, appears to me quite indispensable for the person who would do justice to your clergyman; and I think I may boast myself to be, with all possible vanity, the most unlearned and uninformed female who ever dared to be an authoress.*

Novelists are often pestered by people who want them to write up their ideas instead of the novelists' own. Mr Clarke persisted, refusing to take the hint. Perhaps Jane might like to write *'an historical romance illustrative of the august house of Coburg...'.*
Jane replied politely:

> *...I am fully sensible that an historical romance founded on the house of Saxe Coburg, might be much more to the purpose of profit and popularity than such pictures of domestic life in country villages as I deal in. But I could no more write a romance than an epic poem. I could not seriously sit down to write a serious romance under any other motive than to save my life; and if it were indispensable for me to keep it up and never relax into laughing at myself or at other people, I am sure I should be hung before I had finished the first chapter. No, I must keep to my own style and go on in my own way...*

This was official correspondence. Writing privately to Cassandra on 14th February 1813, she allows herself less modesty and more sarcasm. Of *Pride and Prejudice* she says:

> *...I am quite vain enough, and well satisfied enough. The work is rather too light, and bright, and sparkling; it wants shade; it wants to be stretched out here and there with a long chapter of sense, if it could be had; if not, of solemn*

> *specious nonsense, about something unconnected with the story; an essay on writing, a critique on Walter Scott, or the history of Buonaparte.*

She advised her niece Anna Austen: *'Three or four families in a country village is the very thing to work on'* (9th September 1814), and advised her not to send her characters to Ireland, where the manners might be different. She was concerned with accuracy: *'I learn from Sir J. Carr that there is no Government House in Gibraltar. I must alter it to the Commissioner's',* she wrote to Cassandra on 24th January 1813. To a nephew she summed up her work as *'the little bit (two inches wide) of ivory on which I work with so fine a brush'* which produces *'little effect after much labour'.* (To J. E. Austen-Leigh, 16th December 1816.)

Jane Austen's skill as a miniaturist has always been acknowledged. During the twentieth century, her reputation has risen steadily, as the view that she was complacent about a trivial society has given way to the view that she savagely satirizes it. But the charge that she did not respond to, or reflect, the events of her day has echoed from the Prince Regent's librarian down to the present day. My argument is that she reflects social and economic change, and that her wit and satire take as their material the responses of her characters to these changes. She has also often been accused of snobbery. Readers have been misled by her use of words like 'breeding' and 'decorum' which in her day meant merely politeness or good manners. Other readers dislike the indubitably conservative tendency in her books. The present book sets out to clear her of the charges of pettiness, triviality and snobbery and to explain her conservatism by setting it in its historical context. Better understood, she may be seen as a conservationist rather than a die-hard reactionary.

Both the American and French Revolutions occurred within her first twenty-five years. When she was a year old, Britain lost the American colonies in their War of Independence. In 1777 the radical Horne Tooke was sent to prison for advertising for subscriptions for the relatives of Americans *'murdered by the King's troops at Lexington and Concord'.* Loss of the colonies was a blow: the American colonial trade was estimated to bring Britain two million pounds a year. It was hardly surprising that when the Rev. James Woodforde preached *'against the rebel Americans'* on 13th December 1776, the church was full.

On 21st July 1791, Parson Woodforde noted in his diary:

> *Shocking accounts in the papers of dreadful riots at Birmingham, Nottingham, etc., on account of commemorating the French Revolution the fourteenth of this month. The Presbyterian and Independent Meeting houses pulled down to the ground, and the inside furniture burnt, many of the Dissenters' houses destroyed, amongst the rest Dr Priestley's, both town and country houses burnt.*

Radicals and left-wingers were jubilant. Thomas Holcroft wrote to William Godwin (1756–1836, author of *Political Justice,* 1793, a proposal for Utopian communism): *'Hey for the new Jerusalem! The millennium!'*

The upper classes trembled and called for law and order. Horace Walpole (1717–97) wrote to Hannah More on 23rd March 1793: *'Religion, morality, justice, have been stabbed, torn up by the roots; every right has been trampled underfoot.'* On 9th February that year he had written to her of '...*a crime that passes even the guilt of shedding the blood of poor Louis—to hear of atheism avowed, and the avowal tolerated by monsters calling themselves a National Assembly!'* He wonders whether *'civilisation can be recovered, or the republic of Chaos can be supported by assassination'.*

Jane Austen's own cousin, Eliza de Feuillide, was the wife of a French count who lost his head on the guillotine in 1794. The widow came back to England and married Jane's brother Henry. Henry was the nearest thing in the energetic Austen family to a ne'er-do-well; having failed at banking, he became a clergyman. He seems to have made Eliza happy.

Writing with hindsight the year Jane Austen died, the poet Percy Bysshe Shelley (1792–1822) said in his preface to *The Revolt of Islam* (1817):

> *The French Revolution may be considered as one of those manifestations of the general state of feeling among civilised mankind produced by a defect of correspondence between the knowledge existing in society and the improvement or gradual abolition of political institutions. The year 1788 may be assumed as the epoch of one of the most important crises produced by this feeling. The sympathies connected with that event extended to every bosom. The most generous and amiable natures were those which participated the most extensively in these sympathies. But such a degree of unmingled good was expected as it was impossible to realise.*

The Abbey Gateway, Reading. Inside was the school where Jane and Cassandra went in 1785. The Austen girls, however, did not stay more than a few months. This watercolour drawing by an unknown artist dates from about 1800. (Reproduced by permission of the British Library, Ms 28676 f. 388)

If the revolution had been in every respect prosperous, then misrule and superstition would lose half their claims to our abhorrence, as fetters which the captive can unlock with the slightest motion of his fingers, and which do not eat with poisonous rust into the soul. The revulsion occasioned by the atrocities of the demagogues, and the re-establishment of successive tyrannies in France, was terrible, and felt in the remotest corner of the civilised world.

The hopes of the revolution had been betrayed and *'gloom and misanthropy have become the characteristics of the age in which we live. This influence has tainted the literature of the age with the hopelessness of the minds from which it flowed'.* The dreams of a generation for a better world had turned sour.

Thomas Love Peacock, in his satirical novel *Nightmare Abbey* (1818), which makes fun of (among other things) the poet Shelley himself, makes the character Mr Flosky (who represents the poet Samuel Taylor Coleridge, 1772–1834) say: *'The French Revolution has made us shrink from the name of philosophy, and has destroyed in the most refined part of the community ... all enthusiasm for political liberty.'* Among the educated, which at that time broadly corresponded with the propertied classes, there was an anti-progressive backlash.

Jane Austen belonged to *'the most refined part of the community'*. Readers have not generally found her books *'tainted'* with *'hopelessness'*, but she had good reason for her horror of all things French. She had never had any hopes for revolution. She preferred stability, which seemed to her necessary for civilization. Refugees were pouring in from France. The novelist Fanny Burney married one of them when she was thirty-nine. Her father, the distinguished musician Dr Burney, was distressed by the match, because M. D'Arblay had no money; but the marriage was happy and there was a little boy.

Horace Walpole wrote to Hannah More in a letter dated 26th January 1795:

> *May we have as much wisdom and courage to stem our malevolent enemies, as it is plain, to our lasting honour, we have had charity to the French emigrants, and have bounty for the poor who are suffering in this dreadful season.*

That year, the season was indeed *'dreadful'*; sheep froze to death in the fields.

Britain had to produce more food. Population was increasing — estimates vary between nine million and eleven million in 1800. After the shock of the French Revolution came the rise of Napoleon in 1799, with his expansionist and aggressive policies. The 1800 harvest was disastrous. Fanny Burney saw respectable journeymen's children begging from door to door for halfpence. Imported food supplies were dependent on the course of the war; battles were fought to establish, or to break, naval blockades.

The days of subsistence farming by cottagers were coming to a close. Influential voices had argued earlier that common wastelands, where the poor grazed their sheep or cut furzes, must be enclosed to make larger units for the new scientific farming. The larger enclosed fields made possible a proper rotation of crops. They also made possible the use of machines and wage labour. The agriculturalist Arthur Young (1741–1820) noted in his *Autobiography* that the Duke of Bedford had paid £700 for a threshing and grinding machine, powered by a steam engine. During Jane Austen's lifetime, the change to mechanized, large-scale farming was proceeding. Economic gains were great; the human cost was frightful, as country people lost their common land and were forced into dependence on such days' work as was offered.

Oliver Goldsmith's poem, 'The Deserted Village' (1770) sums up the state of affairs earlier on:

> *Ill fares the land, to hastening ills a prey,*
> *Where wealth accumulates, and men decay:*
> *Princes and lords may flourish, or may fade;*
> *A breath can make them, as a breath has made;*
> *But a bold peasantry, their country's pride,*
> *When once destroyed, can never be supplied.*

The village was deserted, of course, as families sought work in the new industrial towns or migrated.

John Byng, traveller and diarist, reported in 1789:

> *The cottagers, everywhere, look wretchedly, like their cows;*
> *and slowly recovering from their wintry distress; deserted*
> *by the gentry, they lack assistance, protection and*
> *amusement; however my landlord says that in May there*
> *are mayers (alias Morrice dancers) who go about with a*
> *Fool, a man in woman's clothes (the Maid Marian), and*
> *music.*

Despite such vestiges of folk-custom and traditional merriment, the harvest suppers when 200 people dined on plate, the regular Christmas dinners given by Parson Woodforde for the '*poor old men of the parish*', with the present of a shilling (5p) each, inflation, bad harvests, unemployment and the loss of traditional privileges added up to wretchedness. The naturalist Gilbert White (1720–93) wrote in *The Natural History of Selborne* (1789):

> *We abound with poor, many of whom are sober and*
> *industrious, and live comfortably in good stone or brick*
> *cottages, which are glazed, and have chambers above stairs;*
> *mud buildings we have none. Besides the employment from*
> *husbandry, the men work in the hop gardens, of which we*
> *have many, and fell and bark timber. In the spring and*
> *summer the women weed the corn, and enjoy a second*
> *harvest in September by hop-picking. Formerly, in the dead*
> *months they availed themselves greatly by spinning wool, for*
> *making of barragons, a genteel corded stuff, much in vogue*
> *at the time for summer wear, and chiefly manufactured at*

> *Alton, a neighbouring town, by some of the people called*
> *Quakers; but from circumstances this trade is at an end.*
> *The inhabitants enjoy a good share of health and longevity;*
> *and the parish swarms with children.*

His picture of a rural economy feeding raw materials to a
nearby town for manufacture, yet with cottage industry
becoming redundant, is characteristic of the period. Gilbert
White lived only a few miles from Chawton.

In 1784 he reports a struggle between the rich and the poor:

> *A very large fall of timber, consisting of about one thousand*
> *oaks, has been cut this spring in the Holt forest; one fifth of*
> *which, it is said, belongs to the grantee, Lord Stawell. He*
> *lays claim also to the lop and top; but the poor ... assert*
> *that it belongs to them, and assembling in a riotous manner,*
> *have actually taken it all away. One man, who keeps a*
> *team, has carried home for his share forty-five stacks of*
> *wood. Forty-five of these people his lordship has served with*
> *actions.*

Landowners saw rebelliousness everywhere and saw to it that
trespasses against property were severely punished. There was
little understanding of the despair and anger of the labourers,
partly because of traditional attitudes and partly because of what
seemed to be the terrible example of revolutionary France.

Mrs Jane West, a writer Jane Austen did not care for, wrote in
Letters To a Young Woman (1806):

> *The contented cottager, quiet, sober, laborious and cheerful,*
> *is fast disappearing from our rustic haunts; wretchedness,*
> *with all its attendant train of vices, or thoughtlessness, and*
> *I may add, insolent extravagance, the result of great gains*
> *and little foresight, supply his place.*

She thought the workers who had moved from the country to the
towns were overpaid and consequently wanting in deference to
their betters.

Farmworkers lived on bread and cheese, with bacon as an
occasional treat. There is evidence that their standard of living
fell during Jane Austen's lifetime. When they could get hold of
meat, they roasted it. Middle-class commentators considered this
shockingly extravagant: when would the poor get it into their
heads that meat would go much further in nourishing soup?

Hannah More (1745–1833), the writer of religious and moral works, was always on the look-out for fecklessness among the poor. She was shocked that there were poor people who spent their money on white bread, good meat and early vegetables while their children went ragged and shoeless. We might think, today, that such people had their priorities right, but Hannah More valued respectable appearances above good food. *'Poor people who have but little regard for appearances will seldom be found to have any great regard for honesty and goodness'*, she wrote in *The Shepherd of Salisbury Plain* (1794). William Cobbett (1763–1835), the Radical journalist, accused her of teaching the poor to starve without making a noise.

The Rev. Thomas Malthus, in *An Essay on the Principle of Population* (1798), commented that it was a

> *matter of great surprise that, notwithstanding the immense sum that is annually collected for the poor in England there is still so much distress among them. Some think that the money must be embezzled, others that the churchwardens and overseers consume the greater part of it in dinners. All agree that somehow or other it must be very ill-managed. In short the fact that nearly three millions are collected annually for the poor and yet that their distresses are not removed is the subject of continual astonishment. . . . But the transfer of three shillings and sixpence [17½p] a day to every labourer would not increase the quantity of meat in the country. There is not at present enough for all to have a decent share.*

(Parson Woodforde's dinners, as recorded in his diaries, always comprised two separate joints of meat, vegetables, puddings and pies.) *'The labouring poor, to use a vulgar expression'*, said Malthus, voicing a complaint still heard today, *'seem always to live from hand to mouth'*. He writes of labourers getting 18 old pence (7½p) a day. During and after the Wars, wages dropped, though prices rose.

In 1801 Arthur Young wrote:

> *Go to an alehouse kitchen of an old enclosed country, and there you will see the origin of poverty and poor rates. For whom are they to be sober? For whom are they to save? . . . For the parish? If I am diligent, shall I have leave to buy a cottage? If I am sober, shall I have land for a cow?*

> *If I am frugal, shall I have an acre of potatoes? You offer
> no motives; you have nothing but a parish officer and a
> workhouse. Bring me another pot of ale.*

The same year, he wrote:

> *Lord Euston is going the tour of Suffolk, ordering returns to
> be made of all carts, wagons, horses, mills and ovens; a step
> preparatory in the expectation of an invasion. But it is in
> everyone's mouth that with such a price of corn half the
> country would join an enemy.*

In 1814 there were riots in London. Arthur Young wrote:

> *Country labourers throughout the kingdom are in the
> greatest distress...from 30 to 40 houses at London have
> had their windows broken, many their doors forced, and
> everything in them destroyed...the military were called
> forth.*

After the War ended in 1815, there was mass unemployment and
bitter discontent. Imported wheat was ruining the farmers.
Rioting was not new. Before the War, George III had been shot
at on his way to open Parliament, to cries of *'Give us peace and
bread'*, *'No king!'*, *'No war!'*. Parson Woodforde was in the
crowd. *'The mob was composed of the most violent and lowest
democrats'*, he wrote.

In *Northanger Abbey*, Eleanor Tilney is mocked by her brother
Henry, who accuses her of picturing

> *to herself a mob of three thousand men assembling in St
> George's Fields; the Bank attacked; the Tower threatened,
> the streets of London flowing with blood, a detachment of
> twelfth Light Dragoons (the hopes of the nation) called up
> from Northampton to quell the insurgents, and the gallant
> Frederick Tilney, in the moment of charging at the head of
> his troop, knocked off his horse by a brickbat from an upper
> window.*[2]

Catherine has been talking of *'horrors'* and Eleanor imagines
she must be talking of a *'riot'*. Henry mockingly fills in the
picture. Yet the scene Henry speaks of was not so different from
many enacted during Jane's lifetime. She does not make
explicit reference to political events, but her novels are peopled
with soldiers at the ready, sailors who fight in decisive battles and

win prize money. We can extract from her novels various threads of social history if we read between the lines.

Social and economic distress combined with radical ideas from across the Channel to threaten the privileged classes. Tom Paine's *The Rights of Man* (1791) sold 200,000 copies in the first year. He followed it up with *The Age of Reason*, which attacked religion. Miners in Cornwall and Newcastle sold their Bibles to buy it.

The prosperous classes were terrified of Jacobinism, which meant radical opinions, French views of liberty, equality, fraternity, rights of man and subversion of the social order. (Jacobinism is not to be confused with that other disloyalty from the Establishment viewpoint, Jacobitism. The Jacobite cause, support for the Stuart kings against the Hanoverian succession, died in 1745 with the defeat of Bonnie Prince Charlie at Culloden.) The Jacobins were a French political club, founded in 1789, in the old convent of the Jacobite friars. The Jacobins preached democracy, the absolute equality of all men. In a society of a few extremely rich people and a great mass of poor, this was an explosive and 'dangerous' doctrine.

View of Southampton around the time when Jane Austen was living there and writing *Elinor and Marianne*, published later under the title *Sense and Sensibility* (The Fotomas Index)

The poet Shelley, who urged the working classes to unite and throw off the yoke, while living on unearned income from his father's estate, was the son of a baronet, educated at Eton and Oxford. Despite his revolutionary politics, which brought him under official government surveillance which was not quite efficient enough to arrest him, he was aristocratic in his outlook. In *A Philosophical View of Reform*, he looked coolly down on the *'new aristocracy'*, made up of *'attornies and excisemen, and directors and government pensioners, usurers, stockjobbers, country bankers with their dependants and descendants'*.

As Shelley observed, the traditional leadership of the landowners was threatened by commercial interests, and both groups were threatened by radical discontent from below. There was resistance to French ideas because the French were then our traditional enemies. But some working-class English people secretly hoped that 'Boney' would win and bring social justice with him. The possibility of a bloody revolution, like the one in France, was an ever-present anxiety.

English society bent, but did not break. Jane Austen's novels *Pride and Prejudice*, *Emma* and *Persuasion* offer an extended analysis of this bending whereby the rising classes were assimilated, if sometimes awkwardly, into the country gentry. The aristocracy, the gentry and the new rich sank their differences and combined against the common enemy—radical protest. It is arguable, too, that heads were saved from rolling by the fear of invasion. Despite internal divisions, society united against a common threat.

Against the new social restlessness and talk of 'rights' there was a long tradition whereby inequality was ideologically justified. It stemmed back in English history to the homilies, or political sermons, dictated by the government and preached from the Sunday pulpits under the Tudors. The homilies supported the divine right of kings and said that questioning the social order was a crime against God and the king, his representative on earth. It was argued that inequality was a necessary framework which, while it might be uncomfortable for individuals, was right and proper for the whole. The system had to be kept working harmoniously.

Dr Samuel Johnson (1709–84), a writer Jane Austen enormously admired, believed that *'rules of distinction of rank ... create no jealousy, as they are allowed to be accidental'*. The theologian, William Paley (1743–1805) wrote:

> *How thankful, then, the poor should be that the very
> circumstances in which they are placed has such a powerful
> tendency to cherish the divine spirit of dependence and
> subordination.*

As was frequently pointed out, wealth brought dreadful temptations with it: the poor were better off, really, as they were. In *Duties of the Female Sex* (1796), the Rev. Thomas Gisborne wrote that girls in danger of the pride of rank should be told that '*differences of rank are not for the advantage of individuals, but for the benefit of the whole*'.

The old doctrine of '*subordination*' in which Dr Johnson believed got a new twist towards the end of the eighteenth century. People who had left the countryside to work in towns had lost contact with the gentry and clergy, who advised them to be content with their lot. Town workers were turning rebellious. W. Coombe writes in *A Word in Season to the Traders and Manufacturers of Great Britain* (1792) that he is surprised that anything like a

> *levelling and equalising spirit should have risen in the
> manufacturing towns: I conceive it to be essential to their
> progress and existence, that the rich inhabitants should be
> few, and the laborious many, and the subordination of the
> different classes, to each other, is the life and soul of every
> species of manufactory.*

These '*new fangled doctrines of the rights of man*' would mean ruin to the rich, who would be '*despoiled of their property*' and the poor would lose their jobs. '*The mad spirit of popular tumult*' was to be dreaded and, if necessary, resisted.

Arthur Young spoke for many when he wrote: '*Everyone but an idiot knows that the lower classes must be kept poor or they will never be industrious.*' Low wages were thought to be good for trade.

Sir F. M. Eden, who travelled England to investigate the state of the poor, and published his findings in 1797, wrote:

> *It is one of the natural consequences of freedom that those
> who are left to shift for themselves must sometimes be
> reduced to want…. Manufactures and commerce are the
> true parents of our national poor.*

Town poverty was largely invisible to the gentry until the popular outcry in the 1840s. Rural distress, which was less radical politically, was visible, and was dealt with piecemeal by the well-meaning, who would have rejected the hard-headed realism of the economist Adam Smith (1723–90). Smith wrote in 1776 that

> *civil government, so far as it is constituted for the security of property, is in reality instituted for the defence of the rich against the poor, or of those who have some property against those who have none at all.*

The principle of subordination, widely held, its arguments endlessly repeated, appealed to those on the comfortable rungs of the social ladder. The rejection of this ideology by the less fortunate is equally understandable.

Although the machine age was ending the system of hereditary rank, which was never, in England, rigidly exclusive, and reorganizing society into competing classes, based on marketable skills, the gentry lived in accordance with the old beliefs of hereditary caste society. Jane Austen accepted these beliefs, but with considerable reservations.

Pamphleteers angrily attacked the impieties of Tom Paine, William Godwin, and Mary Wollstonecraft (author of *A Vindication of the Rights of Woman*, 1792, wife of William Godwin and mother of Mary Godwin who wrote the novel *Frankenstein* and married the poet Shelley). The pamphlet writers hated feminism, atheism and ideas from France and Germany.

Jane Austen's class justified their privileges and comforts by insisting on service and charity. Radically to reshape society was unthinkable (what would become of them?), but they could feel themselves justified in the eyes of God and man if they exercised Christian charity and benevolence. Writers insisted that to be charitable was not only a Christian duty: it was the only way to placate the angry poor and keep them in their place.

Jane West shows her awareness of the political base for virtuous action when she exhorts middle-class girls to be good to the poor for the good of their own souls. She adds, significantly,

> *on the side of the indigent, this social intercourse with their superiors would prove the best check on the democratical spirit that is let loose among them ... prudential*

> *considerations are enforced by the positive duties which we*
> *owe to our superiors, equals and inferiors; thence follow the*
> *obligations of respect, compliance and benevolence.*

The rolling abstractions blur the message: Mrs West is arguing that we must look up to our betters, get along with equals, and be kind to inferiors. She takes it for granted that everybody knows where they stand in the pecking order, although, as we see from the novels of Jane Austen, where resentments arise over precedence and status, this was no longer true. Mrs West was sure that Tom Paine was to blame for the trouble from the rustics, who had lost the *'moral propriety of their opinions and their affectionate attachment to their superiors'*. The servant classes, she complains, cavilled against Providence by questioning *'why one person ought to be richer than another.... Vulgar politicians'* exclaimed against the injustice of people *'permitted to possess wealth'*. And at the least pressure of distress, these people had the impertinence to demand, not solicit, parochial relief. Mrs West hoped society would not be

> *tainted with the leaven of democracy, those mischievous*
> *doctrines which impose on the commonalty, or persuade them*
> *to imagine that the suppression of rank and opulence would*
> *contribute to their own exaltation, or even advantage.*

Levelling down would do nobody any good. Shrill and self-righteous, Mrs West is typical in combining an attack on the workers with insistence on charitable duty. If her readers were not generous and charitable, they would forfeit their claim to be liked.

> *Society has always a claim upon us: they who entirely limit*
> *their attention to their own households, and will neither*
> *open their purses nor their hearts at the call of benevolence,*
> *nor bestow their time and their attention to the demands of*
> *good neighbourhood, must expect to live disliked or despised.*

'Charity', said the Rev. Thomas Gisborne, *'should be looked on as part of common expenses'*, an idea so widely held throughout the nineteenth century as to be a commonplace. *'To employ, from motives of benevolence, those who cannot obtain work elsewhere, is one of the best kinds of charity'*, he adds.

Writing on the *Duties of Men in the Higher and Middling Classes of Society* (1794), Gisborne argued that the private gentleman should charge *'only fair and moderate rents'*. Otherwise his farm might fall into the hands of *'ignorant adventurers, who will exhaust the soil and leave owing rent'*. It was the duty of the landowner to maintain the value of his land, in the public interest. The good landlord should resist the enclosure of open fields and commons, and set an example of duty and generosity.

> *The good landlord does not turn multitudes of industrious poor adrift by converting half a parish into an immense sheepwalk, which no longer affords occupation to one-twentieth part of the former inhabitants, nor by combining many small farms into a few of great size, that he may escape the expense of repairs, or save himself and his agent the trouble of attending to petty accounts.*

He will not be

> *unmindful of the welfare of the infirm and disabled, nor of the children of the lowest classes, not even in those villages and hamlets where his most distant property lies.*

He might try supplying *'corn or coals at reduced prices'* instead of cash handouts. He would contribute to *'friendly societies'* and to the *'weekly and Sunday schools'*.

Such contributions from the better-off were necessary, since the poor and the unemployed could literally starve. There was no social security, no old-age pension, no benefits except *'parish relief'*. For Jane Austen, as we see from the character of Mr Knightley in *Emma*, the duties of the good landlord were many; his fulfilment of them the measure of his moral worth.

Malthus could see no way out of the ecological trap. He believed it was impossible to have a society in which all members

> *should live in ease, happiness and comparative leisure; and feel no anxiety about providing the means of subsistence for themselves and their families....I have read some of the speculations on the perfectibility of man and society with great pleasure....I ardently wish for such happy improve-ment. Mr Godwin has conjectured that the passion between the sexes may in time be extinguished... no progress whatever has hitherto been made,*

he writes with dry wit.

Jane Austen, in a letter written in May 1801, rejected the *'disciples of Godwin'* along with his Utopian communism, as '*disreputable*'. With such books as *Political Justice* and *The Rights of Man* being published, it looked to the middle and upper classes as if there were an international conspiracy to abolish all governments, property and religion. It was with the reaction, that emphasized political conservatism, religious revival and moral reform, that Jane Austen eventually took her stand.

She was more intelligent than the likes of Mrs West, but there is no evidence that Jane Austen dissented from the widespread opinion that individual goodness would save her class from extinction. On the contrary, she accepted the emphasis on charitable crumbs from the rich man's table, if not as a hedge against revolution (an aspect she does not deal with), then as a Christian and social duty. Her heroines go on charitable errands to the poor in their villages.

Writing to Cassandra on 24th December 1798, she says:

> *Of my charities to the poor since I came home you shall have a faithful account. I have given a pair of worsted stockings to Mary Hutchins, Dame Kew, Mary Steevens and Dame Staples; a shift to Hannah Staples, and a shawl to Betty Dawkins; amounting in all to about half a guinea . . .*

At the time half a guinea ($52\frac{1}{2}$p) was the price of a new cloak.

On Sunday 28th November 1812, she writes to Martha Lloyd:

> *We are just beginning to be engaged in another Christmas duty, and next to eating turkeys, a very pleasant one, laying out Edward's money for the poor; and the sum that passes through our hands this year is considerable, as Mrs Knight left £20 to the parish.*

NOTE: All page references to Jane Austen's novels are to the Oxford illustrated edition, edited by R. W. Chapman. Readers are advised to consult this edition if possible, as it is fully annotated and contains a wealth of explanatory background material.
[1] Jane Austen *Pride and Prejudice* p. 43   [2] Jane Austen *Northanger Abbey* p. 113

2

The gentry

Jane Austen wrote to Cassandra on 25th November 1798:

> *You must tell Edward that my father gives 25s [£1.25p] apiece to Seward for his last lot of sheep, and, in return for this news, my father wishes to receive some of Edward's pigs.*
>
> *We have got Boswell's* Tour *to the Hebrides and are to have his* Life of Johnson; *and, as some money will yet remain in Burdon's hands, it is to be laid out in the purchase of Cowper's works.*

The economic news is followed by evidence of her interest in current literature, and this letter faithfully reflects the typical concerns of educated country people. (The *Tour to the Hebrides* was published in 1785, the *Life of Johnson* in 1791 and Cowper's poems in 1782.) Crops and the livestock provided livelihood and therefore were of interest; leisure, however, gave them time for mental cultivation.

The English gentry lived on their estates, spent their money locally, and took the lead in local activities, unlike the French nobility, who made themselves unpopular by absenting themselves. A French commentator, the Comte de Montalembert, noticed that the English gentry did not

> *disdain, as the old French nobility did, to accept administrative, legislative and judicial functions. Far from it—they have almost monopolised them, and by so doing have maintained themselves at the head of all the development of society.*

In England the able man born in humble circumstances could make his own way by talents, energy, industry. The successful business man could buy an estate and join the local gentry, like Mr Weston in *Emma*. In *Pride and Prejudice* Mr Bingley finally buys an estate with the money his father has made in trade.

Social acceptance could be earned, if not for oneself, at least for one's children and grandchildren.

In France the word 'nobles' included both the great aristocrats and the smaller country landowners. In England there was a division into two main groups: the nobility, or titled aristocracy; and the lesser country gentry, the baronets, knights and squires. There was some hostility between the two sets. We see this division, and the mutual hostility, reflected in Jane Austen's books, in particular *Pride and Prejudice* and *Persuasion*. The world of her novels is the world in which she moved, that of the rural gentry and university-educated clergymen, rising as high as a baronet or two *(Sense and Sensibility, Mansfield Park, Persuasion)*.

In *Pride and Prejudice* Darcy is the nephew of an earl, and the Elliot family in *Persuasion* are related to Viscountess Dalrymple and her daughter. But in the main, her characters are landowners of medium-sized estates, untitled country gentlemen who inherit the land, with younger brothers who have their livings to earn in the Church, the law, the Army or the Navy. The girls have no prospects but marriage. The owners of country estates, who lived on rents and the sale of timber, were the people who counted. (The French word *rente* means income, a reflection of those conditions.) But the economic, if not the social, dominance of the traditional gentry was being challenged by the new wealth made in trade and commerce. The well-connected squires and professional people Jane Austen belonged to and writes about are shown in her books coming to terms with the pressures of social change. Emma fails to make this adjustment; Sir Walter Elliot in *Persuasion* never accepts that young men from nowhere can earn distinction by service in the Navy, but his daughter Anne goes forward into the future as the wife of a successful naval officer.

These social changes carried with them shifts in values and behaviour, so the old standards were cast in doubt. With so many new people about, you could no longer be certain who was and who was not 'a gentleman'. This is a key issue in Jane Austen's books. As we shall see, the idea of a gentleman was not restricted to externals, but ran right through the character, like lettering through Blackpool rock. Characters in Jane Austen struggle with social or economic difficulties and through the experience of living discover, some of them painfully, the nature of true gentility. For Jane Austen this is indistinguishable from virtue or morality. (See Chapter 3.)

Cities had Nash terraces and elegant squares like this one, but were filthy and surprisingly noisy, with '... strolling players, Punch and Judy men, vendors of fresh spring water, quack medicines, charms, ... the scavenger with his cart ...' who all 'jangled bells of variable hideousness'. (Letter to the *Public Advertiser*, 23 October 1783) This watercolour by T. Gingal shows the north side of Portman Square, Bath (The Fotomas Index)

The rank of gentleman implied responsibilities as well as privileges. William Cobbett distinguished between '*a resident native gentry, attached to the soil, known to every farmer*' and '*a gentry only now and then residing there at all, looking to the soil only for its rents, viewing it as a mere object of speculation*'. Jane Austen's worthy landlords, notably Mr Knightley in *Emma*, stay on their estates when possible and administer them efficiently. In *Mansfield Park* Sir Thomas Bertram, as soon as he is home from seeing to his business interests on his West Indian estate in Antigua, gets down to the business of estate management. The restless Henry Crawford, on the other hand, is indicated as irresponsible in that he is an absentee landlord. His subsequent elopement with another man's wife has been prepared for by this shadow on his character.

Jane Austen's view was that of Lord George Bentinck, who said:

> *I believe that the first ingredient in the happiness of the people is that the gentry should reside on their native soil, and spend their rents among those from whom they receive them.*

Jane Austen's characters are typical of eighteenth-century society in that they are country people, who visit town only occasionally. The root of the system was *primogeniture*, by which the eldest son inherited his father's land and social position, while the younger ones (except where family means allowed for provision) had to fend for themselves. (See Chapter 7.)

> *The enthusiastic fondness of the English for the country*, wrote the American ambassador, Richard Rush, *is the effect of their laws.... Scarcely any persons who hold a leading place in the circles of their society live in London. They have* houses *in London, in which they stay while Parliament sits, and occasionally visit at other seasons; but their* homes *are in the country. Their turreted mansions are there, with all that denotes perpetuity — heirlooms, family memorials, pictures, tombs. This spreads the ambition among other classes, and the taste for rural life, however diversified or graduate the scale, becomes widely diffused. Those who live on their estates through successive generations, not merely those who have titles, but thousands besides, acquire, if they have the proper qualities of character, an influence throughout their neighbourhood. It is not an influence always enlisted on the side of power and privilege. On the contrary, there are numerous instances in which it has for ages been strenuously used for the furtherance of popular rights.*

In the nineteenth century the new commercial and manufacturing rich lived in town, visiting the country for sport. However, the picture is not clear cut: Bath was only one of several provincial centres of fashion and amusement.

Merchants and financiers were important in the changing economy, but the society they had to adapt themselves to was dominated by the values and traditional lifestyle of the hereditary landowners. Merchants, after all, had been buying estates since the fifteenth century.

Eighteenth-century people held much the same view of the matter as the Roman writer Cicero. He was much read in the period, both in the original Latin and in translation. *The Offices*, dealing with the duties of privilege and with moral obligation, was recommended to, and read by, many well-brought-up young men and women.

Cicero writes:

> *The career of a merchant is only to be despised if pursued on a small scale, but if it includes large and valuable transactions and imports from all over the world resulting in a large clientele from honest dealing, it is not so much to be condemned; in fact, if those who indulge in it become satisfied ... with their profits, and retire ... to their country estates ... this seems to be entirely commendable. But of all the sources of income the life of a farmer is the best, pleasantest, most profitable and most befitting a gentleman.*

To have made one's money in trade was not so good as having inherited it, socially speaking, and people had more chance of social acceptance if they retired from business before settling in the country. In *Pride and Prejudice* Jane Austen shows the new-rich Bingley sisters as snobbish and spiteful, whereas Elizabeth's Uncle and Aunt Gardiner, who have a warehouse in the city and are busily engaged in commerce, are *'intelligent'*, *'gentlemanlike'*, even *'elegant'*.

Elizabeth's father, Mr Bennet, is a small country squire; Darcy is a great landowner of enormous wealth and an aristocratic background. Elizabeth makes a great social leap in marrying him. This is one of the reasons Lady Catherine, Darcy's aunt, is against the match. Elizabeth, despite *'low connections'* on her mother's side, reminds Lady Catherine that as a *'gentleman's daughter'* she can claim to be an eligible wife for Mr Darcy. Elizabeth bristles with resentment when patronized by Lady Catherine. Lady Catherine, like other upper-class women of her time, takes upon herself the right to visit those of lesser rank without considering whether or not such calls are convenient. She drops in on the Bennet family and goes about opening doors in the hall and peeping into rooms without being invited. She annoys Elizabeth Bennet with such rudeness yet, if Lady Catherine had been visiting a cottage, nobody would have been surprised.

Superciliousness was resented. Parson Woodforde wrote in his diary for 7th November 1783:

> *Lady Jernigan is a fine woman, but high and mighty ... upon the whole we spent an agreeable day, but must confess that being with our equals is much more agreeable.*

In Henry Fielding's novel *Tom Jones*, Squire Western is provincial and loutish, uncultured and brutal. He hates the great aristocrats: '... *the lords ... I heate the very name of* themmun'. While the coolness towards the aristocracy was still alive in Jane Austen's time, the rougher country types had apparently disappeared.

In 1808, R. L. Edgeworth remarked that things had changed:

> *The Sir Wilful of Congreve, the Western of Fielding, and the Tony Lumpkin of Goldsmith, are not now to be found in the most remote part of England. The ignorant, hunting, drunken, obstinate, jovial freedom-loving tyrant is no more to be seen, except in the old novels and plays. The ptarmigan, the bustard, the cock of the woods, and the country squire, are nearly extinct. Instead of country squires we now have country gentlemen.*

It was during the eighteenth century that the great collections we now consider characteristic of the 'stately home' were made, and manners had become more polished to match the new elegance in living. (See Chapter 3.) The Grand Tour, increased wealth, better roads and more frequent travel, especially to London, all contributed. The man of wealth was now expected to be a man of taste.

In 1814 P. Colquhoun published *A Treatise on the Wealth, Power and Resources of the British Empire*. He estimates the first class of society (royal and aristocratic) as 576 families; the second class of '*baronets, knights, country gentlemen and others having large incomes*', with their families at 6,861. This, of course, is the class to which Jane Austen's characters in the main belong, although her own position was in the third class: '*dignified clergy, persons holding considerable employments in the State, elevated situations in the law, eminent practitioners in physic, considerable merchants, manufacturers on a large scale, and bankers of the first order*', an estimated 12,200 families.

The fourth class, totalling 233,650 families, are those from whom Jane Austen's characters often prefer to keep their distance:

> *persons holding inferior stations in church and state, respectable clergymen of different persuasions, practitioners of law and physic, teachers of youth of the superior order, respectable freeholders, ship owners, merchants and manufacturers of the second class, warehousemen and respectable shopkeepers, artists, respectable builders, mechanics and persons living on moderate incomes.*

The fifth, sixth and seventh classes go down to *'idle and disorderly persons, supported by criminal delinquency'*. The Army and Navy seem to escape classification, but officers of the Army, Navy and Marines including all officers on half pay and the superannuated, with their families, totalled 10,500; they certainly would not go below the fourth class. The Navy—Jane Austen's brothers became admirals—was more open to ability than the Army where commissions were for purchase. (See Chapter 7.) Colquhoun's figures have been much disputed, but they are less interesting to us than the relative status ascribed to his groupings. Two-thirds of the House of Commons at that time were landowners; the other hundred or so were in trade or the armed services; they were mostly connected by birth with the aristocracy. Yet in 1726 Daniel Defoe, in *The Complete English Tradesman*, noted that tradesmen's children rose to be *'gentlemen, statesmen, Parliamentary men, privy counsellors, judges, bishops and noblemen'*. Having succeeded in 'moving up the ladder', they then proceeded to consolidate their positions by buying land, marrying heiresses, or both.

MANSFIELD PARK

Sir Thomas Bertram, owner of Mansfield Park, is a baronet. The Bertrams have a town house as well, but give it up, and Lady Bertram lives entirely in the country, *'leaving Sir Thomas to attend his duty in Parliament'*.[1] Lady Bertram, formerly Miss Maria Ward, of Huntingdon, with *'only seven thousand pounds'*, has done very well for herself to catch Sir Thomas, with a handsome house and large income.

> *All Huntingdon exclaimed at the greatness of the match, and her uncle, the lawyer, himself, allowed her to be at least three thousand pounds short of any equitable claim to it.*[2]

Sir Thomas, with an estate in the West Indies, one at home and a seat in Parliament, has an active, busy life, not the life of the idle rich: Lady Bertram, however, spends all day on the sofa with her fringe and her dogs. She earns our amused contempt, but we are meant to respect her son Edmund: *'there was a charm, perhaps, in his sincerity, his steadiness, his integrity'*.[3] While his father and elder brother are abroad, Edmund fills his father's place as head of the family, *'in carving, talking to the steward, writing to the attorney, settling with the servants'*.[4]

Malvern Hall by John Constable (1776–1837). Contemporary readers would have visualized Mansfield Park as much like this; a gracious mansion in a spacious park, with statues on either side of the porch, old trees in the grounds and a peacock on the lawn. (Sterling and Francine Clark Art Institute, Williamstown, Massachusetts)

Edmund's cousin Fanny Price, sent home to Portsmouth, thinks nostalgically of Mansfield, where *'elegance, propriety, regularity, harmony ... peace and tranquillity'* reign. At Mansfield

> *everybody had their due importance; everybody's feelings were consulted. If tenderness could ever be supposed wanting, good sense and good breeding supplied its place.*[5]

While order and politeness are not the whole of life, they are still worth something. In Fanny's noisy, untidy, messy Portsmouth home, she does the correct thing and introduces Henry Crawford to her father. Mr Price stops swearing, *'such was his instinctive compliment to the good manners of Mr Crawford'*.[6]

But Henry Crawford, as Fanny knows, and Sir Thomas painfully finds out, is merely well mannered. He is unprincipled. He does not bother about his Norfolk estate, although he suspects his agent is not efficient. But when he is making up to Fanny, he

> *introduced himself to tenants, whom he had never seen before; he had begun making acquaintance with cottagers whose very existence, though on his own estate, had been hitherto unknown to him.*[7]

This is a black mark against Mr Crawford: responsible landlords behave more like Sir Thomas, whose *'wonted concerns'* are

> *to see his steward and his bailiff—to examine and compute—and in the intervals of business, to walk into his stables, and his gardens, and nearest plantations.*[8]

Although not so rich as Sir Thomas, Mr Crawford is comfortably off, with £4,000 a year. He considers that Edmund will be *'pretty well off'* with *'seven hundred a year…a fine thing for a younger brother; and as of course he will still live at home, it will be all for his* menus plaisirs [pocket money]…'.[9] Edmund has already told Henry's sister, Mary, that he is one of the *'younger sons who have little to live on'.*[10]

Mary retorts: *'You would look rather blank, Henry, if your* menus plaisirs *were to be limited to seven hundred a year.'* Her implied rebuke to Henry's careless selfishness is just, yet she herself, as Fanny observes, *'had only learnt to think nothing of consequence but money'.*[11] She disarms criticism by frankness about her mercenary intentions, but betrays herself constantly. Eventually even Edmund sees through her.

Early on, Mary fails to understand the economy of the countryside. She tries to get her harp carried by a farm cart at harvest-time, and is surprised to find them all in use.

> *'Coming down with the true London maxim, that everything is to be got with money, I was a little embarrassed at first by the sturdy independence of your country customs'.*[12]

As Dr Johnson said: *'When the power of birth and station ceases, no hope remains but from the prevalence of money'.* The Crawfords are parasites. Jane Austen's heroines are charitable, her gentlemen useful. She is often accused of snobbery, yet she clearly disapproves of gentlefolk who are not energetic and responsible leaders. She is sympathetic to yeoman farmers and small professional men, respectable businessmen who are not quite gentry, if they are worthy and sensible.

Mr Rushworth, despite his magnificent estate and his £12,000 a year, was '*an inferior young man, as ignorant in business as in books, with opinions in general unfixed, and without seeming much aware of it himself*'.[13] Mr Rushworth is the only son, so inherits. The Rev. Thomas Gisborne, in his *Duties of Men in the Higher and Middling Classes of Society* (1794) warns that parents should teach their younger children

> to look forward without repining to the customary superiority of the eldest, and the eldest to regard it without arrogance and emulation, by inculcating in them all, that distinctions of rank and employment visibly tend to the common good.... The eldest son of a private gentleman seldom pursues any profession, he notes.

Mary Crawford, who would like to marry Edmund Bertram, frankly wishes he were the future baronet, instead of a mere younger brother. The Crawfords disturb the peace of Mansfield, but are not allowed to destroy it. Mr Rushworth, Tom Bertram, Henry Crawford, are all unworthy of their privileges. Jane Austen looks forward to moral leadership in the Mansfield world from Edmund, after he has been ordained priest.

Mrs Norris, Lady Bertram's sister, takes upon herself the old aristocratic rôle of prescribing medicines for the poor; she claims to have cured the coachman's rheumatism and offers the gardener at Sotherton a charm for the '*ague*' (fit of shivering, with high temperature) she has diagnosed.[14]

Samuel Richardson's Pamela, in the novel of that name published serially between 1740 and 1744, said modestly:

> I am not so good as the old ladies of former days who used to distil cordial waters, and prepare medicines, and dispense them themselves.

Yet, although Pamela suggests the tradition was dying, George Eliot's aristocratic Mrs Cadwallader, in *Middlemarch*, set in the late 1820s, keeps up the custom.

Mrs Norris keeps a sharp eye on the servants. We are not told how many Mansfield employs, but we find out that Aunt Norris admires the housekeeper's strict régime at neighbouring Sotherton, where Maria Bertram goes as Mr Rushworth's bride.

> '*That Mrs Whitaker is a treasure! She was quite shocked when I asked her whether wine was allowed at the second*

> *table, and she has turned away two housemaids for wearing white gowns'.*[15]

Fanny Price's mother, Mrs Norris's sister, lives in comparative squalor in Portsmouth. Yet even she has two servants, although she cannot manage either of them.

Arthur Young writes in his *Autobiography*:

> *I remember one day at dinner Judge Wills saying to his wife, 'My dear, I think we are rather scant in servants' — yet there was one to every chair and some to spare.*

Elizabeth Mure, in *Some Observations of the Change of Manners in My Own Time, 1700–1790*, says that in her youth *'one man servant was thought sufficient for most families, or two at most, unless they kept a carriage which was a thing uncommon in those days, and only used by the nobles of great fortune'*.

Early in the century there is evidence that even great ladies superintended their own kitchens, laundries and dairies. Mrs West reports that one such received a proposal of marriage while starching a ruff. Later such practical tasks were considered beneath the dignity of a lady. New wealth meant that more girls set up to be fine ladies: farmers' daughters, in particular, were criticized for their pretensions. They came under attack from writers for playing the piano, dressing up and refusing to help their mothers with the chores. But the chores still had to be done, and there were no labour-saving gadgets, no electricity to help cut down the time spent on housework.

Jane Austen herself, looking for a home in Bath in 1801, wrote on 12th May to Cassandra:

> *My mother looks forward ... to our keeping two maids ... we plan having a steady cook and a giddy young housemaid, with a sedate, middle-aged man, who is to undertake the double office of husband to the former and sweetheart to the latter.*

From the apparently prim Miss Austen, this is really rather a naughty joke.

It appears from the novels that servants could be sent running about with messages in all weathers, when it was too severe for their mistresses to leave the house, even for church. As Mary Wollstonecraft tartly observed in *A Vindication of the Rights of Woman* (1792):

> *The lady who sheds tears for the bird starved in a snare,*
> *and execrates the devils in the shape of men, who goad to*
> *madness the poor ox, or whip the patient ass, tottering under*
> *a burden above its strength, will nevertheless keep her*
> *coachman and horses whole hours waiting for her, when the*
> *sharp frost bites, or the rain beats against the well-closed*
> *windows.*

Life for the few was ample and comfortable. The rest had to do
the best they could.

PERSUASION

Horses, then the only means of transport, were as
central to the economy as oil is to ours. They were also used for
pleasure, in riding and hunting. Horses and sport are a major
concern of Jane Austen's less intelligent and worthy male
characters. Sport does not preoccupy her heroes: they are
responsible, busy landowners (Sir Thomas Bertram, in *Mansfield
Park*, Mr Knightley in *Emma*), dutiful clergymen (notably
Edmund Bertram in *Mansfield Park*). Captain Wentworth in
Persuasion is a successful seaman. His maturity is contrasted with
the footling triviality of Charles Musgrove, married to Anne's
petulant sister Mary.

> *A woman of real understanding might have given more*
> *consequence to his character and more usefulness, rationality*
> *and elegance to his habits and pursuits. As it was, he did*
> *nothing with much zeal, but sport; and his time was*
> *otherwise trifled away, without benefit from books, or*
> *anything else'.*[16]

Jane Austen's opinion of breeding animals in order to kill
them is made clear in a devastating sentence which, almost
casually, sums up the more futile aspects of the life around her:

> *The Mr Musgroves had their own game to guard, and to*
> *destroy; their own horses, dogs and newspapers to engage*
> *them; and the females were fully occupied in all the other*
> *common subjects of housekeeping, neighbours, dress, dancing*
> *and music.*[17]

The guarding and destroying of game was a rich man's
privilege, and aroused passionate social antagonism. When
Anne's father, Sir Walter Elliot, lets his home, Kellynch Hall, to

Admiral Croft, Sir Walter's agent tells him that the Admiral *'would be glad of the deputation, certainly, but made no great point of it; — said he sometimes took out a gun, but never killed ...'.*[18] One wonders, then, what the Admiral was shooting at.

'The deputation' is worth some explanation. By an Act of 1671, nobody was allowed to kill game except owners of land worth £100 a year, the eldest sons of esquires (a rank between that of a knight and a gentleman) or persons of higher degree. These were the people *'qualified'* to kill game, and they could kill it anywhere they chose, on anybody's land.

Although their eldest sons were *'qualified'*, esquires and *'persons of higher degree'* were not all qualified by their property holdings to shoot. The lord of the manor could give the right to kill game to his gamekeepers, but not to his younger sons, unless he made them gamekeepers *'by deputation'*. Younger sons actually took jobs as gamekeepers to get the right to shoot.

In *The Spectator*, No. 122 (20th July, 1711), Sir Roger de Coverley describes a man with a spaniel at side as *'a yeoman of about an hundred pounds a year, an honest man: he is just within the game-act, and qualified to kill an hare or a pheasant: he knocks down a dinner with his gun twice or thrice a week: and by that means lives much cheaper than those who have not so good an estate as himself. He would be a good neighbour if he did not shoot so many partridges ...'*

In No. 131 (31st July, 1711), we read:

> *It is usual for a man who loves country sports to preserve the game on his own grounds, and divert himself upon those that belong to his neighbour ... the country gentleman, like the fox, seldom preys near his own home.*

Colonel Peter Hawker records in his diary for 11th January 1811 that during his journey from Longparish in Hampshire to Exeter, which took nineteen hours, *'not being post day, the mail stopped whenever we saw game, and during the journey I killed four partridges. When it was too dark to shoot, our party mounted the roof, and sang choruses.'*.

The farmers grumbled. They were not permitted to kill the game their fields and hedgerows harboured, no matter how pestiferous, and had to persuade a qualified member to shoot it for them. Thomas Bewick the engraver (1753–1828), wrote in his *Memoir* that *'as the farmers feed the game, it would only appear to be an act of justice to secure the game to the farmers as their exclusive property'*.

But no such law was passed. A servant might '*beat bushes*' for his master, and so might a stockbroker, attorney, surgeon, '*or other inferior person*' if invited to do so by a qualified sportsman, but they might not take part in the actual killing of game. It was against the law to sell game.

By an Act of Parliament, 1808, the law was modified, so that landowners could give the '*deputation*' to whomever they chose; this annoyed traditionalists, who resented the encroachment of 'unqualified' sportsmen. Mr Rushworth grumbles about it.

Such laws of course led to a black market. Poachers became professional criminals. Cases were so numerous that magistrates were given powers of summary conviction.

These restrictions explain why fox-hunting was more popular. It was not then socially exclusive, but open to anybody who had a horse and could ride it. In Jane Austen's time, hunting was a new and fashionable sport. In *Mansfield Park* the Bertrams and Henry Crawford go fox-hunting, as well as shooting. The game laws were finally relaxed in 1831, under the reforming Whig Government.

Lord Chesterfield sneered at the '*rustic illiberal sports of guns, dogs and horses which characterise our English bumpkin country gentlemen*'. He was writing in the mid-eighteenth century, the time of Squire Western in *Tom Jones*. On 28th February 1749, Lord Chesterfield wrote to his illegitimate son:

A gentleman goes duck-shooting, an engraving by Thomas Bewick (1753–1828). He thought farmers ought to be entitled to shoot the game on their own land. (Syndics of Cambridge University Library)

There are some pleasures that degrade a gentleman as much as some trades could do. Sottish drinking, indiscriminate gluttony, driving coaches, rustic sports, such as fox-chases, horse-races, etc., are in my opinion, infinitely below the honest and industrious professions of a tailor and a shoemaker which are said to deroger [degrade].

The duel, to 'defend one's honour' by proving one's courage, was part of the code of behaviour expected of a gentleman since the sixteenth century. Tradition said it was right

> *... greatly to find quarrel in a straw*
> *When honour's at the stake.*[19]

As part of the general refinement of manners, Beau Nash, the famous master of ceremonies, banned duelling at Bath. The practice declined when men stopped wearing swords, but at the end of the century they were still duelling with pistols.

The Rev. Thomas Gisborne described the custom in 1794 as '*irrational, savage and unchristian*'. He hoped that '*common sense and religion*' would '*at last prevail. To give or to accept a challenge is now but a very equivocal proof of courage even in the estimation of those ... termed ... men of honour.*'

Middle-class moralists, like Gisborne, Low Church people, dissenters, Methodists and Evangelicals (including William Wilberforce), the pacifist Quakers, all opposed duelling on rational and religious grounds. Such opposition was coloured by social rivalry, for the broad division in influential society was between the well-born High Church people who owned land, and the ambitious dissenters in trade. Between these groups the struggle for economic and political dominance was waged. But it must be mentioned that Lord Chesterfield and Horace Walpole, both earls, despised the folly of duelling.

Some people went in for high-minded agitation, others mocked, and yet others said the custom was dying out. But there was enough of it going on for the *Anti-Jacobin* in 1805 to deplore its increase. The poet Lord Byron (1788–1824) said he had been involved, as negotiator or 'second' (the combatant's companion, friend and support) in at least twenty quarrels.

A man called Humphrey Howarth turned up for a duel with no clothes on, afraid his wound might fester if the bullet should take in any cloth from his garments. His opponent parted from him in contempt, without shooting.

Duels were fought as a reply to accusations of cowardice and to avenge the seduction (or 'dishonour') of female relatives. In 1803 a duel was fought in Hyde Park with pistols between an Army captain and a girl's brother. Both were killed.

Mrs Jane West, in her *Letters To a Young Woman* (1806) writes crisply of '*those laws of honour which compel the fashionable rake to be an expert swordsman before he aspires to be a seducer*', since seducers had to '*run the gauntlet of husbands, fathers and brothers*'.

SENSE AND SENSIBILITY, PRIDE AND PREJUDICE

Colonel Brandon, in *Sense and Sensibility*, relates that he has challenged and fought Willoughby, who has seduced and abandoned Colonel Brandon's own protégée, daughter of the woman Colonel Brandon has formerly been unhappily in love with. All this is a melodramatic, unconvincing and minor part of the novel, an early one in the canon, second to be written.

By the time Jane wrote her next, *Pride and Prejudice*, the seduction of Lydia Bennet is a disgrace requiring only that she be '*made an honest woman of*' by marriage. Her seducer, Wickham, has to be persuaded to do the right thing by having it made financially worthwhile. Lydia's father gives her the income on her future inheritance of £1,000. There is no serious suggestion in the book that her father, her uncle Gardiner or her friend Mr Darcy should avenge her dishonour by fighting a duel. The hysterical Mrs Bennet is sure Mr Bennet '*will fight Wickham, wherever he meets him, and then he will be killed*',[20] but her relatives calm her down and deal with practicalities.

[1] Jane Austen *Mansfield Park* p. 20 [2] *ibid*. p. 3 [3] *ibid*. p. 65 [4] *ibid*. p. 34 [5] *ibid*. p. 392 [6] *ibid*. p. 402 [7] *ibid*. p. 404 [8] *ibid*. p. 190 [9] *ibid*. p. 226 [10] *ibid*. p. 214 [11] *ibid*. p. 436 [12] *ibid*. p. 58 [13] *ibid*. p. 200 [14] *ibid*. p. 189 [15] *ibid*. p. 105 [16] Jane Austen *Persuasion* p. 43 [17] *ibid*. p. 42 [18] *ibid*. p. 22 [19] Shakespeare *Hamlet* Act 4 scene 4 [20] Jane Austen *Pride and Prejudice* p. 287

3

Decorum and true gentility

The formality, even stiffness, with which Jane Austen's characters speak to one another can create a barrier for modern readers. Awareness of vocabulary changes, however, together with close attention to what the characters actually say, can reveal to us the difference between the language of warm affection and that of frigid politeness.

Many words have changed their meanings: *'candour'* meant not bluntness, but readiness to think the best of people; *'disgusting'* meant merely 'distasteful'.

In *Emma*, *'Mrs Weston and her son-in-law'* means *'Mrs Weston and her stepson'*. The confusion between 'step' and 'in-law' relationships survived as late as Dickens, where Mr Murdstone, David Copperfield's stepfather, is spoken of as his father-in-law.

Mrs Elton speaks of *'my brother, Mr Suckling'*, meaning her sister's husband. The distinction between kinship and connection by marriage was blurred. Emma's sister Isabella is married to Mr Knightley's brother John. *'We are not so much brother and sister as to make it at all improper'*, says Emma, standing up to dance with Mr Knightley.[1]

In *Sense and Sensibility* Willoughby eats a *'nuncheon'* at Marlborough, later explained as a pint of porter (beer) with cold beef: in fact, the kind of pub food we get today, a snack. A *'luncheon'* did not then mean a midday meal; it was another word for a snack. This survived in America as late as 1886. In *The Bostonians* by Henry James, Mrs Tarrant is gently mocked for using the word *'lunches'* for *'any episodical repast at any hour of the twenty-four'*.[2] I am told this usage is still common in Canada.

(Look carefully at the *context* if you are surprised by a word or are unsure of what it means. The *tone* of what is being said will give some clue to meaning or to the strength of feeling behind a word.)

The novelist Kingsley Amis has complained that Jane Austen writes about *'distinctions between a Tweedledum labelled 'well-bred' and a Tweedledee labelled 'coarse''.*[3] Words like *'breeding'* and *'gentleman'* cause one of our chief difficulties in coming to terms with her world.

The very word *'manners'* did not mean quite what it does now: Jane Austen's age believed with the philosopher Hobbes (1588–1679) that manners were *'small morals'*. *'Good breeding'* meant an elegant deportment, politeness, while *'good manners'* involved morality. This was bound up with *'decorum'*, a favourite word with Jane Austen. People she approves of are described as *'gentlemanlike'* (and usually *'sensible'* as well); *'well-bred'* and *'civil'* usually mean only superficially polite.

Jane Austen is constantly testing and defining the terms against the behaviour of her characters, who discuss the nature of 'true gentility', as against the merely external kind, which may turn out to be deceitful.

The word *'breeding'* originally meant education, up-bringing: we use the expression 'badly brought-up'. In French, Spanish and Italian, an ill-mannered person is said to be 'badly educated'. But today the word 'breeding' makes hackles rise: it suggests inherited, unearned prestige, arrogant privilege. We associate the word with genetics, not education.

In Jane Austen's day it meant ordinary politeness and consideration, which were by no means universal, despite the ambition of her contemporaries to appear polished. We see failures in elementary tact and kindness all through her books. Characters who fail in this way are condemned for it.

For Jane Austen, 'good breeding' was not restricted to manners and accent, to external style, although these were expected of her class: it included right feeling and right thinking, as well as correct behaviour.

People considered that the crude and rough manners of preceding centuries, together with stiff aristocratic formality, had been replaced by grace and 'modern ease'. *'The fashionable world is grown free and easy; our manners sit more loose upon us'*, said *The Spectator* in 1711. But if it was overdone, 'ease' could degenerate into rudeness, friendliness into impertinence. Only when we read Jane's work with these values in mind, freeing ourselves from modern anti-élitist prejudices or the foolish notion that manners are a badge of class, can we enter sympathetically into her world and grasp what she is saying.

Sir Richard Steele defined a gentleman in *The Guardian*, No 34, 1713 as having

> *a clear understanding, a reason free from prejudice, a steady judgement, and an extensive knowledge*, and suggested that *he must be modest without bashfulness, frank and affable without impertinence ... principled in religion, instructed in all the moral virtues, and lead through the whole course of the polite arts and sciences.*

The philosopher John Locke (1632–1704) wrote: '*Teach children humility and good breeding will not be wanting.*' His book, *Some Thoughts Concerning Education*, had gone to twenty-five editions by 1777. Jane Austen almost certainly knew it: its influence is diffused through her novels. Locke insisted that good breeding involved '*keeping that respect and distance, which is due to* everyone's *rank and quality*'. It was important to have '*a disposition of mind not to offend others*' and '*that general good will and regard for* all *people, which makes any one have a care not to show, in his carriage, any contempt, disrespect or neglect of them.*'

Lady Sarah Pennington, in *An Unfortunate Mother's Advice to Her Absent Daughters* (1766): '*All ... have a right to civility and good humour from you: a superiority of rank or fortune is no licence for a proud supercilious behaviour.*' She offered her girls a formidable reading list, which included Cicero's *Offices*, essays and letters. These were well known in translation to readers of both sexes.

For Cicero, good manners arise from greatness of soul. The well-bred person avoided '*too much niceness and effeminacy*' on the one hand, '*clownishness*' on the other. Decorum was a code, greater than the sum of the rules, infusing a person's whole being and outlook. Cicero defines it as '*restraint, moderation, temperance, self control*'. It could not be separated from moral goodness:

> *what is right and proper can be conceived at the very root of all virtue ... decorum can be seen in all our deeds, words, and in physical movement and bearing ... reasonableness and self-control ... steadiness ... consideration for others ... logical consistency.*

Jane Austen's contemporary, a Mrs Pole, wrote:

> *There is a particular satisfaction in reading all Miss Austen's works—they are so evidently written by a gentlewoman—most novelists fail and betray themselves in attempting to describe familiar scenes of high life, some little vulgarism escapes and shows that they are not experimen-*

tally acquainted with what they describe, but here it is quite different. Everything is natural, and the situations and incidents are told in a manner which clearly evinces the writer to belong *to the society whose manners she so ably delineates.*

The period produced numerous books of conduct, advice to young men and women: Dr Fordyce's *Sermons*, Gisborne's *Duties of Men in the Higher and Middling Classes* and his *Duties of the Female Sex*, Jane West's *Letters to a Young Man* and *Letters to a Young Woman*, Mrs Hester Chapone's *Letters on the Improvement of the Mind* and Mrs Sarah Trimmer's periodical, *The Guardian of Education*, are well-known examples.

Although some of these books touch on etiquette and deportment, in the main they deal with morality and religion. There is little practical advice of the kind we find in nineteenth-century compilations.

Adam Petrie, an unemployed clergyman working as tutor in a great house in Scotland, published a book in 1720 called *Rules of Deportment and of Good Breeding*. It starts:

Civility is a pleasant accomplishment, a duty enjoined by God. We are commanded to be courteous to all men, and to give honour to whom honour is due.

He repeats medieval and Renaissance instructions not to scratch the ears or blow the nose with the fingers, mingled with moral precepts backed by Biblical texts.

Later writers keep the morality and drop the practical exhortations. The books have a sameness which soon becomes wearisome. There are severe warnings against vanity, particularly when it leads to the sin of imitating one's betters in dress; the reader is urged instead to think of her (usually her) immortal soul. Young women are told they must exercise vigilance against their sexual passions, the enemy lurking within. Many of these tracts were written by clergymen, but others were written by women out to contradict the audacious feminist Mary Wollstonecraft.

Jane West is unusual, yet symptomatic of her time, in that her arguments for traditional morality are supported, in addition to scriptural reference, by instances drawn from the new studies of comparative anthropology and archaeology. Her teaching, though, is conventional.

> *Rudeness of habit* [poor clothing] *is soon cast aside*, writes
> Mrs West, *rudeness of manner is more adhesive . . . . Though
> wealth and commerce have rendered the* externals *of a
> gentlewoman so attainable, that she is no longer to be
> distinguished by her habit ; it is left to the more patient and
> less prosperous times to transcribe the complaisance,
> affability, condescending attention to the claims of others,
> love of propriety and regard of decorum, which are the
> essentials.*

The word *'condescending'* was used without sarcasm. Fordyce and
all the others preach against improper pride of rank.

Lord Chesterfield defined good breeding as the ability *'to
converse with ... inferiors without insolence, and with ... superiors
with respect and ease'*. Adam Petrie wrote: *'It is most insolent and
undecent to be familiar with superiors ... yet to be familiar with an
inferior is obliging and civil.'* This may have been useful advice in
1720, when there was greater agreement as to who inferiors and
superiors were. But during the intervening eighty years there had
been, as we have seen, a great deal of social climbing. There were
frequent complaints that people no longer knew or kept their
rightful places.

The distinction between the gentry and the middle class was
not entirely one of birth, nor of education, nor of manners : it was
a blend of all of them, and thus open to discussion. Foreigners
found the nuances hard to grasp, because the same professions
included some who were gentlemen and some who were not.

'Vulgar' mothers who embarrass their more refined daughters
are characteristic of a society in a state of flux, as Jane Austen's
letter to Cassandra on 24th September 1805 shows:

> *I called yesterday morning (ought it not in strict propriety
> to be termed yester-morning?) on Miss Armstrong and was
> introduced to her father and mother. Like other young ladies
> she is considerably genteeler than her parents. Mrs
> Armstrong sat darning a pair of stockings the whole of my
> visit. But I do not mention this at home, lest a warning
> should act as an example.*

The grand connections in the Austen family came from the
maternal side. Mrs Austen was sometimes found digging
potatoes. Her lack of concern for appearances was clearly a cause
of anxiety to her daughters.

SENSE & SENSIBILITY

Manners today are easier and less formal than in Jane Austen's day, yet reading *Sense and Sensibility* we find plenty to shock us. So much crude familiarity, all the tormenting and teasing of poor Marianne about boyfriends, seems astonishing from people of Jane Austen's class. Can it really have been like that, we wonder?

Jane Austen is saying that it was, and that she disliked such behaviour. The message is that true gentility (and the word genteel was not used sarcastically) was a combination of outward politeness and inner goodness of heart. On this all the moral writers agreed.

Sir John Middleton's hearty kindness grates on Marianne's raw nerves. Elinor makes the best of things. Lady Middleton is cold-hearted, but polite; her mother, Mrs Jennings, is loud, tactless and cheerful, but kind and generous. Lady Middleton wishes her mother, whose money comes from trade, would drop her old city friends. When Mrs Jennings's other son-in-law, Mr Palmer, publicly calls her *'ill-bred'*, she laughs it off. Even the fastidious Marianne comes to recognize that Mrs Jennings is a good woman. Her heart is in the right place, which makes her worth three of the correct, but selfish, characters like her daughter, Lady Middleton, and the mercenary Fanny Dashwood.

Mrs Jennings says the Dashwood girls can go out *'with one of my daughters'* and Charlotte Palmer offers to chaperon them *'any time till I am confined'*.[4] (The cheerful way Charlotte and her mother Mrs Jennings rattle on about Charlotte's pregnancy embarrasses Lady Middleton.) Chaperonage in Jane Austen's day, however, was not the strict surveillance it became in Victorian times, when no respectable middle-class girl could be left alone with a man, or seen out anywhere without a female servant or companion.

The etiquette of engagements was complicated. To enter into a secret engagement was wrong and deceitful. But once committed, either secretly or publicly, a young man could not honourably break the engagement; he had to wait for the girl to release him. Only an engagement allowed correspondence.

Everybody can see that Marianne is in love with Willoughby. Elinor feels their mother should sort things out by asking Marianne whether or not they are engaged. Mrs Dashwood thinks it would be indelicate to ask. Elinor suggests (and Jane

Austen seems to agree) that Mrs Dashwood is failing in her duty. But *'common sense, common care, common prudence were all sunk in Mrs Dashwood's romantic delicacy'*.[5]

When Elinor sees Marianne writing to Willoughby, however, Elinor is persuaded they must be engaged. She is unaware that Marianne is being recklessly indiscreet. Elinor, believing Willoughby to be Marianne's fiancé, is deeply angry at his cruel letter shaking her off; she is amazed that he acknowledges *'no breach of faith'*.[6]

But Marianne breaks the illusion that there was an engagement: *'He is not so unworthy as you believe him.'*[7]

Shaking hands was a mark of particular regard, a gesture of friendship or even commitment. Marianne shakes hands with Edward Ferrars to welcome him as a brother-in-law. The gesture was almost as warm as a kiss would be today. Understanding this, we find no anti-climax in Marianne's anguished plea: *'Good God! Willoughby, what is the meaning of this? Have you not received my letters? Will you not shake hands with me?'*[8] But, as we have seen, she should not have written to him.

Among young women, the use of Christian names was a mark of warm friendship, not to be used until acquaintance was formed. In Jane Austen's three earlier novels, *(Northanger Abbey, Sense and Sensibility, Pride and Prejudice)* young women speak of men by their surnames alone. It is assumed by most commentators that a shift in manners occurred before the others were written. Young men spoke to each other by surnames alone, a recent change. Thomas Moore, in his *Memoirs of R. B. Sheridan* (1825) said the custom had disappeared whereby young men *'of high station'* called each other *'by such familiar names as Dick, Jack, Tom, etc.'*.

Dr R. W. Chapman's notes comment that young men addressed each other *'as they do now'*. This annotation is itself now out of date: we must amend this to *'as they did until the second world war'* and point out that this custom obtained only in the middle class and upwards, and most obviously in the grammar schools and public schools of the time.

Within families, children spoke to their parents as either 'sir' and 'madam' or, in affection, as 'mama' and 'papa'. Jane Austen, writing to Cassandra, says *'my mother'*, not 'our mother'; it seems that to say just 'mother', 'aunt' or 'uncle' on their own was considered vulgar. Elinor, exhorting Marianne to pull herself together, says (strangely, to modern ears, since the girls are sisters), *'Think of your mother'*. 'Aunt' and 'Uncle' were followed by the surname, not the Christian name. Mrs Jennings speaks of *'My daughter Middleton'* where we should expect either the formal *'my daughter, Lady Middleton'* or her first name.

ENTERTAINING AND VISITING

The Dashwoods, living on the edge of genteel poverty, entertain generously — it was expected of the gentry. Edward is *'earnestly pressed'* to stay more than a week. Callers are invited to dinner as a matter of course.

During the eighteenth century, the dinner hour moved from noon to six-thirty (in very smart society). Most of Jane Austen's characters dine at four.

During dinner the custom of *'cross-toasting'*, in which one guest rises and names another with whom he would *'like to take wine'* was used. Some have said that the custom died in the nineteenth century, but it was practised in the Forest of Dean in the mid-1950s.

After formal dinner, the sexes divided. The women 'withdrew' to the 'withdrawing' or 'drawing room', while the men lingered over the port. The traveller François de la Rochefoucauld, staying with the Duke of Grafton in 1784, noted that the men used a chamberpot, kept in the sideboard, in front of the company without embarrassment. The men in Jane Austen's time trickled in to the drawing room one by one, although later it was the custom for the host to say *'Shall we join the ladies?'*. Tea and coffee were served in the drawing room.

The time between breakfast (ten o'clock) and dinner was called 'morning'; the word 'afternoon' was hardly used.

'Morning calls' or formal visits survived, vestigially, until after the Second World War. The polite minimum in Jane Austen's time was fifteen minutes. In Parson Woodforde's time, in the 1780s, guests often stayed about an hour, but when Elizabeth Gaskell wrote *Cranford* (1853), it was not polite to stay longer than a quarter of an hour. The etiquette of calling is laid down by Adam Petrie in 1720:

> *If a person that's a stranger in the country settles in it, he is not to visit his equals until they have visited him ... but he may pay his dutiful respects to his superiors, providing that they are not far above his station.*

When people went to stay, the visits stretched to weeks, or even several months at a time. Sir John Middleton lives in '*hospitality and elegance . . . scarcely ever without some friends staying with them in the house*'.[9]

Marianne feels that the rent of the cottage is too high if it includes the duty to suffer boredom at the park. The men talk politics, discuss breaking horses and enclosing land. (John Byng wrote: '*As a sportsman, I hate enclosures, and, as a citizen, I look on them as the greedy tyrannies of the wealthy few to oppress the indigent many.*') We do not know what Jane Austen, or her male characters, thought on this question, although John Dashwood complains that enclosing Norland Common drains his income.

The women compare the heights of their children, a theoretical pursuit, since the children are absent. '*No poverty of any kind, except of conversation, appeared.*'[10]

Good conversation was the mark of good society. Jane Austen's letters frequently complain of '*dullness*' and '*stupidity*'. ('Stupid' meant boring.) She saw the realities of her society clearly enough. In *Emma* we read of

> the usual rate of conversation; a few clever things said, a few downright silly, but by much the larger proportion neither the one nor the other—nothing worse than every day remarks, dull repetitions, old news and heavy jokes.[11]

Mrs West writes:

> . . . though in this age of equalisation one rank slides into another in the article of dress, luxury and amusement, conversation still preserves its aristocratical distinctions . . . the company wait, with the nonchalance of good breeding, till some cockney misapplication of the W, or provincial inversion of the aspirate, determines the stranger's tribe and latitude.

She recommends '*truth and sincerity*' and being a good listener. Good conversationalists should aim '*neither to offend nor to mislead*' and they should not giggle, nor pull faces.

On 24th September 1804 Jane Austen wrote to Cassandra:

> . . . she is very conversible in a common way; I do not perceive wit or genius, but she has sense and some degree of taste, and her manners are very engaging. She seems to like people rather too easily.

Lord Chesterfield's letter of 12th October 1748, defines 'good company' as consisting chiefly

> *of people of considerable birth, rank, and character; for people of neither birth nor rank are frequently, and very justly, admitted into it, if distinguished by any particular merit, or eminency in any liberal art or science ... some even of indifferent characters and morals make part of it. But, in the main ... people of infamous and blasted characters are never admitted ... people of the very first quality can be as silly, as ill-bred, and as worthless, as people of the meanest degree. On the other hand, a company consisting entirely of people of very low condition, whatever their merits or parts may be, can never be called good company.... A company wholly composed of men of learning, though greatly to be valued and respected, is not meant·... they cannot have the easy manners and tournure of the world, as they do not live in it.... Good company is composed of a great variety of fashionable people, whose characters and morals are very different, though their manners are pretty much the same.*

Nearly twenty years later, in a letter to his godson and eventual heir, another Philip Stanhope, Lord Chesterfield amplifies his original definition. In the letter, which is dated 1765, he writes:

> *Do not think I mean, by low company, people of low birth; for birth goes for nothing with me, nor, I hope, with you; but I mean, by low company, obscure, insignificant people, unknown and unseen in the polite part of the world, and distinguished by no one particular merit or talent....*

The economist Adam Smith (1723-90), wrote in his essay, 'Theory of Moral Sentiments':

> *Those who have been educated in what is really good company. not in what is commonly called such, who have been accustomed to see nothing in the persons whom they esteemed, and lived with, but justice, modesty, humanity, and good order, are more shocked with whatever seems to be inconsistent with the rules which those virtues prescribe.*

PERSUASION

Anne Elliot says to her cousin:

> '*My idea of good company, Mr Elliot, is the company of clever, well-informed people, who have a great deal of conversation; that is what I call good company.*'
>
> '*You are mistaken,*' said he gently. '*That is not good company, that is the best. Good company requires only birth, education and manners, and with regard to education is not very nice. Birth and good manners are essential; but a little learning is by no means a dangerous thing in good company, on the contrary it will do very well.*'[12]

Mr Elliot turns out to be a smooth hypocrite, whose pleasant manners conceal a calculating heart. But on social realities we may trust his word.

Persuasion was Jane Austen's last completed novel, unrevised when she died. In it, she submits the ideas of 'good breeding', 'gentility' and 'decorum' to searching analysis. Her satire on Sir Walter Elliot and his daughters Mary and Elizabeth, who claim respect for birth alone, is savage. Their moral emptiness is cruelly exposed.

Their friend Lady Russell is a sympathetic character, but her limitations are clearly marked. What Jane Austen writes of her cannot fairly be applied to the writer herself:

> ... *she had prejudices on the side of ancestry; she had a value for rank and consequence, which blinded her a little to the faults of those who possessed them. She was most correct in her conduct, strict in her notions of decorum, and with manners that were held a standard of good breeding. She had a cultivated mind, and was, generally speaking, rational and consistent.*[13]

Lady Russell's prejudice on the side of ancestry has nearly disastrous consequences. Yet she is far from negligible; only by the very highest standards is she shown to be wanting.

Anne's father, Sir Walter, and her sister Elizabeth, have a '*heartless elegance*' which '*gives a general chill*'; Elizabeth says '*the proper nothings*'.[14] After the Elliots move to Bath because living there is cheaper, Anne sighs '*that her father should feel no degradation in the change; should see nothing to regret in the duties and dignity of the resident landholder*'.[15]

Elizabeth walks *'immediately after Lady Russell out of all the drawing-rooms and dining-rooms in the country'.*[16] *'Country'* means 'area'. Elizabeth's high precedence shows that the Elliots mix only with people like themselves, rural gentry.

> *Silly affronts are taken on points of precedence,* wrote Gisborne, *because a lady is ushered into a room, or taken out to dance a minuet, before another who deemed herself superior, the company is thrown into confusion, and lasting hostilities take place. Yet often, the whole assembled body of heralds would have been perplexed to decide the question.*

Anne's sister Mary Musgrove resents not being given *'the precedence that was her due'* when they dined at the Great House with other families.[17] Her sister-in-law wishes somebody would give Mary a hint.

> *'It would be a great deal better if she . . . would not be always putting herself forward to take place of mamma. Nobody doubts her right to have precedence of mamma, but it would be more becoming in her not to be always insisting on it'.*[18]

Anne is constantly distressed by the heartless snobbery of her father and sisters. When Sir Walter and Elizabeth pay servile deference to their cousins, the Dalrymples, Anne, *'who had never seen her father and sister before in contact with nobility'*,[19] is ashamed of them. Although the Dalrymples belong to the peerage, Anne finds them intrinsically uninteresting. She is embarrassed because she suspects that Viscountess Dalrymple and her daughter consider the Elliots pushy bores.

Against the cold-hearted formality of the Elliots is set the bluff common sense of Admiral Croft and his wife, who rent Kellynch Hall from Sir Walter.

> *Admiral Croft's manners were not quite of the tone to suit Lady Russell, but they delighted Anne. His goodness of heart and simplicity of character were irresistible.*[20]

> Anne *'considered her father so very fortunate in his tenants, felt the parish to be so sure of a good example and the poor of the best attention and relief'* that *'she could not but in conscience feel that they were gone who deserved not to stay, and that Kellynch-hall had passed into better hands than its owners'.*[21]

In these two paragraphs are summarized Jane Austen's true social values. The satire in *Persuasion* is at the expense of snobbery, shown in varying degrees by Sir Walter, his daughters Elizabeth and Mary and their friend Lady Russell. Sir Walter is also a selfish and irresponsible landowner. Jane Austen shows in these lines that she herself is on the side of feeling, and of energy, when it is responsibly channelled.

EMMA

Jane Austen's Mr Knightley is the ideal landowner, the character who is presented as admirable, with no qualifying ironies. He is truly the book's hero. His judgment is always to be trusted. He says in Robert Martin's defence that '*his manners have sense, sincerity, and good humour to recommend them; and his mind has more true gentility than Harriet Smith could understand*'.[22]

Emma tells Harriet that whereas Mr Weston is blunt and Mr Knightley has a '*downright, decided, commanding sort of manner*', Mr Elton is a model of good manners: '*he is good-humoured, cheerful, obliging and gentle*'.[23]

This shows how wrong Emma can be, for Mr Elton is self-seeking, petty and spiteful, as well as conceited. Emma is protected by her wealth from reality. When Mr Elton announces his engagement, Emma decides that '*setting aside the £10,000*' Miss Hawkins did not appear '*at all Harriet's superior*'.[24] But of course Mr Elton would never think of setting aside the money: his aim had been to marry well. He fulfils Mr Knightley's prediction that he would act rationally, even if he did talk sentimentally; he does not throw himself away.

Mrs Elton's manners are certainly bad: she fishes shamelessly for compliments: '*How do you like my gown?*'[25] Emma calls her '*a little upstart, vulgar being, with her Mr E., and her caro sposo ... and all her airs of pert pretension*'.[26]

Mr Knightley is kind, generous and thoughtful to Miss Bates, who is ageing and poverty-stricken. Emma insults her because she is boring, and Mr Knightley reduces Emma to tears by his anger.

Mr Knightley gets about on horseback and often on foot. Emma expects him to live up to his position, but he has too much good sense for show. He has a carriage, but keeps no carriage horses.

Mr Knightley is a busy resident landlord, active about parish business, and a magistrate. The duties of magistrates were wider than today; they included many functions of local government, as Gisborne makes clear. Of magistrates, he writes:

> *In the expenditure of county rates, or other public money, on the construction or repair of gaols, bridges, roads and similar works, let him in each case faithfully and economically apply the sum to its proper object.*

Gisborne hopes the magistrate will not grant licences to too many public houses. In them plots were hatched, *'from the pilfering of a solitary hovel and the petty plunder of an unguarded hen-roost, to highway robbery and midnight murder'*. Public houses were responsible for *'private distress and public insecurity; hence the multitude of our poor, and fulness of our prisons'*.

Poultry-thieving was common: Mr Knightley marries Emma earlier than planned and moves in with Mr Woodhouse because Mrs Weston's hen-roost has been robbed. Mr Woodhouse, confusing pilfering with housebreaking, panics.

The Justice of the Peace, continues Gisborne, needed *'calm attention and unwearied diligence in investigating the cases brought before him, and perfect integrity in deciding them'*.

The poor had to apply to overseers like Mr Knightley and Mr Elton to obtain 'parish relief'. Mrs Elton complains that her

Mr Knightley proposes to Emma. (*Emma* p. 430) (Illustration by Hugh Thomson for the 1911 Macmillan edition)

Miss Bates with Mr Weston and Jane Fairfax behind her with Mr Frank Churchill, arriving at the ball at the Crown. (*Emma* p. 322) (Illustration by Hugh Thomson for the 1911 Macmillan edition)

husband is always at the beck and call of magistrates, overseers and churchwardens. This gives us some idea of the 'parish business' Mr Knightley is always so busy with, at the Crown, with the vicar and Mr Weston and Mr Cole, with Mr Cox the lawyer.

Miss Bates talks of John Abdy, former parish clerk, now bedridden:

> '... *poor John's son came to talk to Mr Elton about relief from the parish; he is very well to do himself, being head man at the Crown, ostler and everything of the sort, but still he cannot keep his father without some help.*'[27]

Emma is aware that she does not contribute what she ought to the '*scanty comforts*' of Mrs and Miss Bates. For the really poor, she sends pitchers of broth out from Hartfield and '*always gave her assistance with as much intelligence as good will*'.[28]

But the limitations of Emma's benevolence are ironically charted by Jane Austen. Emma cannot interest herself in the social welfare of the whole village as Mr Knightley does. She considers he must be happy, living by himself, '*with his farm, and his sheep and his library, and all the parish to manage*'.[29] He is a conscientious administrator. He

> *had generally some point of law to consult ... about ... and as a farmer ... he had to tell what every field was to bear next year ... the plan of a drain, the change of a fence, the felling of a tree, and the destination of every acre for wheat, turnips or spring corn.*[30]

At home, he is *'either reading ... or settling his accounts'*.[31] Mr Knightley, like other country gentlemen, has a collection of coins and medals, fossils and pictures, to entertain visitors with.

Henry Mackenzie wrote in *The Lounger*:

> *The crest of noble or illustrious ancestry has sunk before the sudden accumulation of wealth in vulgar hands. ... Elegance of manners ... dignity of deportment ... pride of virtue have given way to the tide of fortune, which has lifted the low, the illiterate and the unfeeling, into situations of which they were unworthy.*

Emma would have accepted this analysis. Jane Austen looks deeper. She distinguishes between the worthy and the unworthy among the well born as well as among the newcomers.

One suspects that D. H. Lawrence was writing about people like Emma rather than about Jane Austen when he wrote in *Sex, Literature and Censorship (A propos of Lady Chatterley's Lover)*:

> *In the old England the curious blood-connection held the classes together. The squires might be arrogant, violent, bullying and unjust, yet in some ways they were at one with the people, part of the same bloodstream. We feel it in Defoe or Fielding. And then, in the mean Jane Austen, it is gone. Already this old maid typifies 'personality' instead of character, the sharp knowing in apartness instead of knowing in togetherness, and she is, to my feeling, thoroughly unpleasant, English in the bad, mean, snobbish sense ....*[32]

I argue that it is unjust to blame Jane Austen for her acuteness in recording the divisions which were arising in the society around her, as if she were herself to blame for them. Mr Knightley is, with *'no ceremony about him'*, completely a gentleman. He stands for the *'common bloodstream'*, doing his best to heal the artificial breaches Emma wants kept open. Mr Knightley is shown doing his duty in that station of life to which providence has called him.

[1] Jane Austen *Emma* p. 331   [2] Henry James *The Bostonians* (Macmillan, 1886 and Penguin)   [3] Kingsley Amis 'Whatever happened to Jane Austen?' Reprinted in *Jane Austen*, ed. Ian Watt ('Twentieth Century Views' series, Prentice-Hall, 1963)   [4] Jane Austen *Sense and Sensibility* p. 110   [5] *ibid.* p. 85   [6] *ibid.* p. 184   [7] *ibid.* p. 186   [8] *ibid.* p. 176   [9] *ibid.* p. 32   [10] *ibid.* p. 233   [11] Jane Austen *Emma* p. 219   [12] Jane Austen *Persuasion* p. 150   [13] *ibid.* p. 11   [14] *ibid.* p. 226   [15] *ibid.* p. 138   [16] *ibid.* p. 7   [17] *ibid.* p. 46   [18] *ibid.* p. 46   [19] *ibid.* p. 148   [20] *ibid.* p. 127   [21] *ibid.* p. 125   [22] Jane Austen *Emma* p. 65   [23] *ibid.* p. 34   [24] *ibid.* p. 183   [25] *ibid.* p. 324   [26] *ibid.* p. 279   [27] *ibid.* p. 383   [28] *ibid.* p. 86   [29] *ibid.* p. 225   [30] *ibid.* p. 100   [31] *ibid.* p. 312   [32] Harry T. Moore (Ed.) *Sex, Literature and Censorship* (Viking Press, 1959) p. 109

4

Enough to live on

Enclosures earlier on and the rise of manufacturing industry had changed the nature of farming and the patterns of employment. Malthus commented in 1798:

> *The employment of much of the most fertile land in grazing, the improvements of agricultural instruments, the increase of large farms, and particularly the diminution of the number of cottages throughout the kingdom, all concur to prove, that there are not probably so many persons employed in agricultural labour now as at the period of the Revolution. Whatever increase of population, therefore, has taken place, must be employed almost wholly in manufacture, and it is well known that the failure of some of these manufactures, merely from the caprice of fashion, such as muslins instead of silks, or of shoe-strings and covered buttons, instead of buckles and metal buttons, combined with the restraints in the market of labour arising from corporation and parish laws, have frequently driven thousands on charity for support ...the increase of wealth in late years has had no tendency to increase the happiness of the labouring poor.*

As Professor Asa Briggs has pointed out, in the eighteenth century people spoke, in Biblical phrase, of 'the poor', in the nineteenth, of 'the lower orders' and in the twentieth of 'the working class'.

Thomas Bewick, the engraver, was born in 1753. Looking back in his maturity in his *Memoir*, he writes of the independent cottagers of his childhood:

> *These men and their offspring might truly be called 'a bold peasantry, their country's pride'—their children were neither pampered nor spoiled—and to this day ...I think I see their broad shoulders and their hardy sunburnt looks, which altogether bespoke the vigour of their constitutions. These cottagers ...were of an honest and independent*

> *character while . . . they held the neighbouring gentry in the*
> *greatest estimation and respect, and these again in return*
> *did not overlook them but were interested in knowing that*
> *they were happy and well.*

But all this changed during the French Wars.

> *Estates rose in value to an extraordinary height and the*
> *price of grain, etc., still more so. The shipping interest*
> *wallowed in riches; the gentry whirled about in aristocratic*
> *pomposity; they forgot what their demeanour and good,*
> *kind behaviour used to be to those in inferior stations in life,*
> *and seemed now far too often to look upon them like dirt.*

The poet William Wordsworth (1770–1850), wrote a letter in
1817, the year Jane Austen died, to Dugald Stuart:

> *I see clearly that the principal ties which kept the different*
> *classes of society in a vital and harmonious dependence upon*
> *each other have, within these thirty years, either been*
> *greatly impaired or wholly dissolved. Everything has been*
> *put up to market and sold for the highest price it would*
> *buy. . . . All . . . moral cement is dissolved, habits and*
> *prejudices are broken and rooted up, nothing being*
> *substituted in their place but a quickened self-interest.*

Whether or not relations between the different classes were so
ideal during the earlier part of the century, the economic system
was changing, population was shifting, and links were being
broken. Thomas Carlyle, in 1833, coined the phrase *'the cash
nexus'*: the only link binding man to man was now economic.

Landowners still ate their own mutton and beef, bread and
beer, eggs and vegetables, but clothing and shoes were now
bought, even by the poor, instead of being cobbled up at home.
Farm servants and apprentices less often 'lived in'. Self-
sufficiency was made out-of-date by manufacture and trade; the
estate as an economic unit was under pressure; timber was
prematurely felled to pay bills. (See Chapter 9.) Trade increased
through the eighteenth century.

THE SLAVE TRADE

Merchants and financiers sought status by buying
estates but did not wholly rely on them for income. Capital was

Godmersham Park, in Kent, the seat of Thomas Knight, the rich relative who adopted Jane's brother Edward. Such estates needed an income of several thousand pounds a year to keep up, but were themselves producers of wealth. (The Fotomas Index)

still invested in manufacture and commerce and, indeed, in the slave trade.

A good deal of British prosperity in the eighteenth century was bound up in overseas trade. First Bristol and then Liverpool, the western ports, gateways to the Atlantic, grew and prospered from the triangular trade. There was a clear link between the growth of cotton manufacture in Lancashire and the plantation economy of the southern United States built on slave labour. Bristol and Liverpool shipowners made fortunes from the trade in slaves across the Atlantic, the import of raw cotton and the export of British manufactured goods. There was also the trade with the British colonies in the West Indies where slavery and a plantation economy produced sugar for the European market. The typical West Indian landowner was an absentee landowner. Sir Thomas Bertram was, perhaps, unusual in that he actually visited his Antigua estates. It was more common to employ agents and factors and enjoy, in English country comfort, the income. The pattern was, in some respects, similar to that of the absentee landlord in Ireland.

The West Indian sugar economy was, in particular, in decline towards the end of the eighteenth century. Clearly, there was more money in cotton. But sugar beet was beginning to compete with cane. Cane, indeed, was expensive. Plantations, even with slaves, were inefficiently run. Yields were low and becoming lower through overcropping. The economic arguments for slavery, such as they were, became weaker just as the Evangelical movement was arousing the conscience of Britain to the moral arguments against slavery. Even so, the anti-slavery movement faced entrenched attitudes. Admiral Nelson, for example, had no time for the abolitionists: the *'triangle'*, he said, was *'the nursery of seamen'*.

Other people felt this was an expensive way to train sailors. The Rev. Thomas Gisborne was outraged. He wrote in 1794 that *'the blood spilled and iniquities committed upon the coast of Africa'* was *'a traffic repugnant to the fundamental principles of justice, and bidding defiance both to the spirit and the precepts of Christianity'*. Opposition to the slave trade had originated in the 1760s, when a handful of Quakers had courageously protested against the cruelty of the system which was making Britain rich. The poet Cowper, whom Jane Austen admired, abominated the trade.

Gradually the movement gathered force and enrolled all the Low-Churchmen, the Evangelicals and Unitarians (see Chapter 11) and the freethinkers, or agnostics. William Wilberforce, a serious and religious person, tried every year to get Parliament to abolish the slave trade. In 1791 he might have won, but the French slaves rebelled in San Domingo. British feelings ran high, because of the threat to their prosperity. The slave run was eventually abolished in 1807, but slaves at work within the British Empire were not freed till 1833.

In 1814, when *Mansfield Park* was published, slaves were no longer being shipped by Britain, but it is safe to assume that Sir Thomas Bertram's estates in Antigua were worked by black slave labour. We are not told what crops he grew, or the reason for his *'recent losses on his West India estate'*[1] but we know such anxieties were general. After Sir Thomas has sorted his affairs, he comes back to Northamptonshire via Liverpool, but on a 'private vessel', not one of the many cargo boats.[2] After his return from Antigua, we are told in passing that Fanny questions him about the slave trade.

When the Napoleonic Wars ended in 1815, Britain had become a trading power, and a capitalist society. Throughout Jane Austen's lifetime, industry and trade were creating new wealth.

EMMA

In *Emma*, the heroine's vision is bounded by a narrow and exclusive snobbery which is corrected by experience and by Mr Knightley (and thus, implicitly, by the author). Emma objects to the young farmer, Robert Martin, as a husband for her friend Harriet Smith, because she considers it would be impossible to meet him socially.

> '*The yeomanry are precisely the order of people with whom I feel I can have nothing to do. A degree or two lower, and a creditable appearance might interest me; I might hope to be useful to their families in some way or other. But a farmer can need none of my help, and is therefore in one sense as much above my notice as in every other he is below it.*'[3]

Emma, who has £30,000, assumes that Mr Martin '*will be a completely gross, vulgar farmer—totally inattentive to appearances and thinking of nothing but profit and loss*'.[4]

The yeoman did not quite rank as a gentleman, but belonged to the '*middling sort*'. Mrs Jane West, who elected herself mouthpiece for the middle class, was the wife of a yeoman farmer, but there was a vice-admiral somewhere in the family. Her husband's mother's relatives had been rectors of Little Bowden in an unbroken chain for 150 years. The spread of connection and range of status in Mrs West's family alone illustrates the fluidity of eighteenth-century society.

Emma imagines her friendship can raise Harriet to eligibility, but this is wilfulness. Her own status is based on wealth and Harriet has nothing much. Old money was better than new, but it was money that counted. Those who had once had some, but had sunk in the world, like the Bates family, for example, continued to be protected by the generosity of their more affluent friends.

Mr Knightley is angry with Emma for making Harriet refuse Robert: '*A degradation to illegitimacy and ignorance to be married to a respectable, intelligent, gentleman-farmer!*'[5]

We know Robert Martin is to be respected, from the letter he writes proposing marriage to Harriet:

> *as a composition it would not have disgraced a gentleman; the language, though plain, was strong and unaffected … it*

was short, but expressed with good sense, warm attachment,
liberality, propriety, even delicacy of feeling.[6]

As Mr Knightley says, Robert *'always speaks to the purpose ; open,*
straightforward, and very well-judging'.[7]

These qualities are to be rated as more important than the
deficiencies Emma finds: *'awkward look and abrupt manner'* and *'a*
voice . . . wholly unmodulated'.[8] Character, in Jane Austen's books, is
always more important than surface polish.

Robert is a tenant, not a landowner, but he is not poor. Harriet
reports that the Martins live very comfortably, with no indoors
man-servant, but otherwise wanting for nothing. Mrs Martin,
she says, has an upper maid who has lived twenty-five years with
her. The testimony of faithful servants is always a valuable
character-reference in Jane Austen's work.

We see Emma making a last-ditch stand against the new
wealth rising all around her. Her attempt at exclusiveness is
handled ironically and shown to be doomed. Emma likes to think
of herself as dominant in the village of Highbury. She is not
pleased to hear that the Coles are giving a dinner party. The precise
socio-economic circumstances are spelt out:

> *The Coles had been settled some years in Highbury, and*
> *were a very good sort of people—friendly, liberal, and*
> *unpretending ; but, on the other hand, they were of low*
> *origin, in trade, and only moderately genteel. On their first*
> *coming into the country, they had lived in proportion to*
> *their income, quietly, keeping little company, and that*
> *inexpensively ; but the last year or two had brought them a*
> *considerable increase of means—the house in town had*
> *yielded greater profits, and fortune in general had smiled on*
> *them. With their wealth, their views increased ; their want*
> *of a larger house, their inclination for more company. They*
> *added to their house, to their number of servants, to their*
> *expenses of every sort ; and by this time were, in fortune and*
> *style of living, second only to the family at Hartfield. Their*
> *love of society, and their new dining-room, prepared*
> *everybody for their keeping dinner-company ; and a few*
> *parties, chiefly among the single men, had already taken*
> *place. The regular and best families Emma could hardly*
> *suppose they would presume to invite—neither Donwell, nor*
> *Hartfield, nor Randalls. Nothing should tempt her to go, if*
> *they did ; and she regretted her father's known habits which*

would be giving her refusal less meaning than she could wish. The Coles were very respectable in their way, but they ought to be taught that it was not for them to arrange the terms on which the superior families would visit them. This lesson, she very much feared, they would receive only from herself; she had little hope of Mr Knightley, none of Mr Weston.[9]

Eventually, Emma feels herself slighted because Mr Knightley and the Westons are invited, and she is not. Her invitation arrives later, and she accepts. The party is large, including another *'unobjectionable country family'*[10] and the local lawyer, Mr Cox. Emma enjoys herself and decides it was a good idea to condescend to the Coles after all. Emma is satirized for her snobbish attitude.

She is, of course, better educated than people like the Coles. Mrs Cole, the new-rich lady, has *'a new grand pianoforte in the drawing room, while I do not know one note from another, and our little girls, who are but just beginning, perhaps may never make anything of it'*.[11] Emma is invited to use it.

Jane Austen's social comedy deserves some analysis. Emma, hoping for the support of Mr Knightley and Mr Weston, in her snobbish exclusiveness, imagines she is keeping up standards. Mr Weston, who has married Emma's governess, Miss Taylor, is not very different from the Coles in background. He was *'born of a respectable family, which for the last two or three generations had been rising into gentility and property'*.[12]

After marrying into the high and mighty Churchill family and being left a widower, he leaves his captaincy in the army and *'engaged in trade, having brothers already established in a good way in London, which afforded him a favourable opening'*. For years he keeps the house in Highbury going, while carrying on in business, and finally manages to buy *'a little estate ... which he had always longed for—enough to marry a woman as portionless as Miss Taylor'*.[13]

When Emma says to Mr Weston's son, adopted by his grand relatives and called Frank Churchill, that Jane Fairfax is doomed to be a governess, Mrs Weston says: *'You get upon delicate subjects, Emma. Remember that I am here.'*[14] Normally Emma is a stickler for social distinctions: she considers Frank Churchill's *'indifference to a confusion of rank, bordered too much on inelegance of mind'*.[15] The weight we are to attach to the concept of '*inelegance*' here is problematical, and calls in question all Emma's values. But because Emma loves her ex-governess, she does not classify her socially in the cool way she does other people.

So when Mrs Elton, the vicar's wife, whose snobbery and pretensions parody and challenge Emma's own, is surprised to find Mrs Weston '*so very lady-like ... quite the gentlewoman*'[16], Emma is furious. Miss Taylor must be acceptable: she, after all, has brought Emma up. Mrs Elton takes the impersonal social view of Mrs Weston as the humble governess, the girl with no money who has married well.

Friction arising from social pretensions and attempts at exclusiveness in a changing society is the staple of comedy in *Emma*. Mr Weston complains of his first mother-in-law that

> '*she had no fair pretence of family or blood ... ever since her being turned into a Churchill she has out-Churchill'd them all in high and mighty claims: but in herself, I assure you, she is an upstart*'.[17]

Mrs Elton responds with an account of some '*upstarts*' called Tupman, near Maple Grove, where her sister and brother-in-law live. They are, she says:

> '*... encumbered with many low connections, but giving themselves immense airs ... a year and a half is the very utmost they can have lived at West Hall; and how they got their fortune nobody knows. They came from Birmingham, which is not a place to promise much, you know .... One has not great hopes from Birmingham ... they evidently think themselves equal even to my brother Mr Suckling ... who has been eleven years a resident at Maple Grove, and whose father had it before him—I believe, at least—I am almost sure that old Mr Suckling had completed the purchase before his death.*'[18]

Mrs Elton claims to have quite a horror of upstarts.

Mrs Elton's speech reveals her as also an '*upstart*', by the old country standards Emma is clinging to. Her brother-in-law's country estate was bought on mortgage, not inherited. Before her marriage, Mrs Elton had been a Miss Hawkins of Bristol, with £10,000. Her father was a tradesman, just about rich enough to be counted as a merchant. Landed gentry like Emma looked down on commercial Bristol, and Bristol looked down on

Birmingham, whose rich people were more recent, less cultured and refined. They did not venture as far as London or Bath. Miss Hawkins of Bristol met her husband at Bath, and considers herself entitled to sneer at Birmingham.

Bristol fortunes were often made in the slave trade. Mrs Elton shows herself touchy on this point when Jane Fairfax mentions her own gloomy future as a governess. *'If you mean a fling at the slave-trade, I assure you Mr Suckling was always rather a friend to the abolition'*,[19] says Mrs Elton. She doesn't talk about her mercantile father; she would rather talk of Mr Suckling of Maple Grove and his *'barouche-landau'*. This was an expensive carriage, a status symbol. It is as if she said *'the Rolls'*.

Mrs Elton, who boasts that her fault in housekeeping is perhaps *'being too careless of expense'*, says that not only can she afford to feed Jane Fairfax at any time, but *'we have carriages to fetch and convey her home'*.[20] Mrs Elton has the pushy self-assertion of new wealth. It is her fortune, not her talents or qualities of character, which has made her an eligible match.

> *'There are a few ... who fancy that pure love will supply a good everyday dinner,'* writes Jane West. *'This rash conclusion ... proceeds from not knowing the value of money, and not from a Spartan renunciation ... their wants are too numerous even for competence; it is not penury, but affluence, which must supply what they call mere* necessary *expenses.'*

Writing in 1806, when day labourers' wages dropped from a shilling (5p) or one shilling and sixpence ($7\frac{1}{2}$p), to half the former amount, she notes that in *'several branches of the woollen trade, common hands may earn two guineas* [£2.10p] *a week'*. Artisans could earn *'enormous wages'* (unspecified).

Servants' wages doubled during Jane Austen's lifetime, but the cost of living is estimated to have tripled. Adam Smith, in *The Wealth of Nations* (1776) praises free trade, widespread use of machinery and the division of labour, all of which, he saw, would create wealth.

But wealth was not always secure. Mrs West attacked competitive display, which she believed was a habit new in the middle classes. She pointed out that

> *'the profits of the professional man die with him ... yet if people so circumstanced will vie in expense with hereditary*

> *wealth ... the consequences'* were *'that which we hourly see,
> in bankruptcies, suicides, helpless widows and destitute
> orphans ... fraud, extortion, and swindling imposition ...
> the madness of gaming houses, and ... the licentious haunts
> of prostitution'.*

Financial instability was commonplace: on the fringes of Jane
Austen's fictional world we see widows and single women
struggling to keep up appearances in reduced circumstances.

SENSE AND SENSIBILITY

Marianne and Elinor argue about a *'competence'*, or
minimum living standard. Elinor thinks grandeur has little to do
with happiness, *'but wealth has much to do with it'*. Marianne is
shocked: *'beyond a competence'*, it does not afford real satisfaction.
Asked by Elinor to define *'a competence'*, Marianne replies, *'...
eighteen hundred or two thousand a year'*. Elinor laughs: 'One *is
my wealth!'*

> *'And yet two thousand a year is a very moderate income,'*
> said Marianne. *'...a proper establishment of servants, a
> carriage, perhaps two, and hunters, cannot be supported on
> less...'.*[21]

Challenged about *'hunters'*, Marianne blushes. She is thinking
of Willoughby, who later deserts her for a richer girl. Willoughby

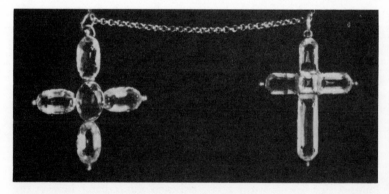

In *Mansfield Park* Fanny Price's young brother William gives her a topaz cross,
but cannot afford to buy a chain. Jane Austen's younger brother Charles got
£30 as his share of the prize-money from a French privateer, and bought his
sisters each a topaz cross and a gold chain. They are in the Jane Austen
museum at Chawton. (J. Butler-Kearney)

plans to give Marianne a horse and she accepts, without considering *'that she must buy another for the servant, and keep a servant to ride it, and ... build a stable'.*[22]

The conversation peters out in dreams of being given a fortune and how it would be spent: the equivalent of *'If I won the pools ...'.*

Elinor, Marianne, their sister Margaret and their mother are living in pinched circumstances, in a cheap cottage, without a carriage. They are of old family, but as children of a second marriage, and mere females with no rights of inheritance, they are less fortunate than their half-brother. He inherits the estate, his own mother's fortune, and marries a rich woman. The girls and their mother have to live on interest, which at 5% brings them a total of £500 a year. Their cottage has four bedrooms and two garrets, and they employ *'two maids and a man'.*

Their half-brother, John Dashwood, makes a deathbed promise to take care of them. John flatters himself with plans to give the girls £1,000 each, but on consideration he whittles it down, first to £500 each, then to *'a present of £50 now and then'* and finally decides he cannot afford to give anything. His wife agrees: she thinks the father probably only meant *'sending them presents of fish and game'.*[23]

They settle in Devon, miles from their home. Their kindly neighbour, Sir John Middleton, fulfils the duties their brother fails in. He sends *'a large basket full of garden stuff and fruit ... followed ... by a present of game'.*[24] Presumably they cannot afford a newspaper; he sends his every day. *The Times* did not circulate far outside London, but Exeter had two local dailies: *Trueman's Exeter Flying Post,' or Plymouth and Cornish Advertiser,* and *The Devon and Exeter Daily Gazette.*

Willoughby, with whom Marianne falls in love so agonizingly, has six or seven hundred a year. He might perhaps have lived on it, but he admits he is *'expensive'* (extravagant) and rejects Marianne for a girl with £50,000.

Marianne finally marries Colonel Brandon, who has £2,000 a year, and becomes *'a wife, ... mistress of a family and ... patroness of a village'.*[25] *'Family'* here means household; *'friends'* is often used in Jane Austen to mean relatives. Marianne takes on a complex of social responsibilities, justifying, in Jane Austen's view, her comfortable place in society.

Elinor is in love with Edward Ferrars, who has only £2,000 of his own. Interest of 5% brought in an income of only £100 a year. Mrs Jennings estimates that if his mother would allow him £500 a year, a couple could live '*snug*' in a cottage with two maids and two men. Without some such financial cushion their prospects are bleak. Edward is to be a clergyman, and Mrs Jennings describes what must have been widespread clerical poverty:

> '*Wait for his having a living! aye, we all know how that will end;—they will wait a twelvemonth, and finding no good comes of it, will settle down upon a curacy of fifty pounds a year, with the interest of his two thousand pounds.... Then they will have a child every year! and Lord help 'em! how poor they will be.... Two maids and two men indeed!.... No, no, they must get a stout maid of all works...*'[26]

Colonel Brandon finally gives Edward a living. But neither Elinor nor Edward is '*quite enough in love to think that three hundred and fifty pounds a year would supply them with the comforts of life*'. This total would be made up from the living (£200), Edward's income of £100, and Elinor's income of £50, the interest on her own capital of £1,000. Eventually Edward's mother allows him something.

The parsonage is described as '*small*', but as it has five sitting rooms on the ground floor and can make up fifteen beds, its upkeep will not be negligible. In the absence of labour-saving gadgets and electricity, domestic help was a necessity in all but the smallest households.

Jane Austen lived with her mother and sister and friend Martha Lloyd on a smaller income than she gave the Dashwoods. Even while her father was alive, Jane wrote to Cassandra on 3rd January 1801: '*My father is doing all in his power to increase his income by raising his tithes, etc., and I do not despair of his getting very nearly six hundred a year.*' Tithes were dues paid by local farmers to the clergy, a tax which was bitterly resented.

Incomes of wealthy gentry in her day have been estimated at between £3,000 and £5,000 a year. This makes her young men with incomes of £12,000 (Mr Rushworth in *Mansfield Park*) or £10,000 (Darcy in *Pride and Prejudice*) very attractive catches indeed. Squires' incomes were from £3,000 down to £1,000, gentlemen from £1,000 down to £300. Jane Austen came low down in the scale.

After her father died in 1805, the family income was only £210 a year. Her rich brother Edward, adopted by a relative, gave them £100; brothers James, Henry and Frank each chipped in £50. The total income was thus £460, on the poverty line for gentry. Less than a quarter of British families had as much as £50 at the time; only a quarter earned more than £200. But by the standards of her class, she was not well off.

In 1807 she writes from Southampton complaining that '*four pair of small soles cost six shillings*' (30p). In the same letter (to Cassandra, 8th February), she says:

> *My mother ... finds she begins the new year with a balance of £30 in her favour ... she began 1806 with £68, she begins 1807 with £99 and this after £32 purchase of stock. Frank too has been settling his accounts ... much increase of house-rent would not do for either. Frank limits himself ... to four hundred a year.*

In 1802, when the Austens moved to Bath, they sold up. Jane wrote to Cassandra on 12th May:

> *Sixty-one guineas and a half for the three cows gives one some support under the blow of only eleven guineas for the*

Jane Austen's drawing room, with her writing desk and keyboard instrument, in her last home at Chawton (J. Butler-Kearney)

> *tables. Eight for my pianoforte, is about what I really expected.... I am more anxious to know the amount of my books, especially as they are said to have sold well.*

People of literary tastes do not sell their libraries except as a last resort.

As an author, she wrote to her brother Francis on 3rd July 1813:

> *You will be glad to hear that every copy of* Sense and Sensibility *is sold and that it has brought me £140 besides the copyright.... I have therefore written myself into £250—which only makes me long for more.*

This sum included the £110 she had made on *Pride and Prejudice*. Her earnings from *Sense and Sensibility, Mansfield Park* and *Emma* totalled £645, so her total during her lifetime makes £755.

She wrote to her niece Fanny Knight on 30th November 1814, that *Mansfield Park*, published that year, might make a second edition.

> *People are more ready to borrow and praise than to buy ... But though I like praise as well as anybody, I like what Edward calls* pewter *too.*

It is not hard to sympathize with her irritation, shown in her letter to Martha Lloyd (16th February 1813):

> *Poor John Harwood! One is really obliged to ... pity ...— and when there is a lack of money, one is on pretty sure grounds.... Charles, that thick-headed Charles, is the best off of the family. I rather grudge him his £2,500.*

When one relates the narrow circumstances in which Jane Austen lived to the affluence of some of her relatives and friends, an affluence partly reflected in her novels, her disgruntled comment becomes understandable.

[1] Jane Austen *Mansfield Park* p. 24   [2] *ibid.* p. 178   [3] Jane Austen *Emma* p. 29   [4] *ibid.* p. 33   [5] *ibid.* p. 62   [6] *ibid.* p. 51   [7] *ibid.* p. 59   [8] *ibid.* p. 33   [9] *ibid.* p. 207   [10] *ibid.* p. 214   [11] *ibid.* p. 215   [12] *ibid.* p. 15   [13] *ibid.* p. 16   [14] *ibid.* p. 201   [15] *ibid.* p. 198   [16] *ibid.* p. 278   [17] *ibid.* p. 310   [18] *ibid.* p. 310   [19] *ibid.* p. 300   [20] *ibid.* p. 283   [21] Jane Austen *Sense and Sensibility* p. 91   [22] *ibid.* p. 58   [23] *ibid.* p. 12   [24] *ibid.* p. 30   [25] *ibid.* p. 379   [26] *ibid.* p. 276

5

The marriage market

You could not shock her more than she shocks me;
Beside her Joyce seems innocent as grass.
It makes me most uncomfortable to see
An English spinster of the middle-class
Describe the amorous effects of 'brass',
Reveal so frankly and with such sobriety
The economic basis of society.

The poet Wystan Hugh Auden wrote these lines about Jane Austen in 1937.[1] The reference is to James Joyce, author of *Ulysses* and *Finnegan's Wake*.

Jane Austen wrote about the tensions between love and money because this was the most acute problem for women of her class in her day. When a woman has no career open to her and thus no power of earning, the choice of a husband becomes more than a matter of pleasing oneself. Jane Austen characters are told it is their duty to marry, if necessary against their inclinations, to relieve their relatives of the burden of keeping them. '*The market is full of well-dressed spinsters*', wrote Jane West. Economic security was not easily obtained: the legitimate object of marriage was to acquire it, combined with emotional security. All Jane Austen's heroines manage it, though none of them finds it particularly easy.

Jane Austen remained single herself, and was sensitive to the temptations created by economic pressure. She jokes about the desperate last-chance marriage of an acquaintance, who had in middle age accepted a Mr Wake:

Maria, good-humoured and handsome and tall,
For a husband was at her last stake;
And having in vain danced at many a ball,
Is now happy to jump at a Wake.

The neat pun is twofold: Maria '*jumps*' now, a hasty and undignified action in pursuit of a husband, compared with dancing; in Ireland a '*wake*' is the gathering that precedes a funeral. The flippant verses have an underlying sadness.

In 1816, the year before Jane Austen died, *The Lady's Magazine* noted:

> *Miss Austin, of Waterfall, near Cork, recovered £4,000 damages, at Cork assizes, against Major Vereker, grand-nephew of Lord Kiltartan, for a breach of promise of marriage.*

Miss Austin (no relation) was clearly felt to have been cheated of considerable expectations, and was compensated proportionately.

A good marriage was the only way to provide for the future. Marriage was a commercial bargain: the middle-class girl's beauty and virtue were up for auction. Mrs West likens female '*fame*', or good reputation, to a '*felucca*' or cargo boat. She writes of the '*delicacy of the merchandise*', of '*pirates, who are ever on the watch to pillage and destroy*'.

Unscrupulous men were not rare. On 16th April 1791, Parson Woodforde wrote:

> *A reward of £100 offered on one of the London papers for apprehending one Richard Perry ... for running away with a Miss Clarke (about 14 years of age) from a boarding school in Bristol. Her fortune great, £6,000 per annum.*

Jane West wrote:

> *The manners of the times, and prevailing style of education, tend to render women at once extravagant and dependent; girls can do nothing to maintain themselves; they must therefore at all events* get husbands ...

But husbands were not so easily got. Men looked round carefully before committing themselves. Arthur Young, in his *Autobiography*, noted about the same time a clergyman with

> *four stout, well-looking, unmarried daughters, that have been marriageable some years. A common spectacle, and everywhere from the same cause; the fornication of men with the abandoned of the sex robs thousands of such virtuous girls of husbands.*

John Byng, in 1788, noted that '*Brighton appeared in a fashionable, unhappy bustle, with such a harpy set of painted harlots, as to appear to me as bad as Bond Street in the spring*'.

Mary Wollstonecraft complained of *'the shameless behaviour of the prostitutes who infest the streets of this metropolis'*. Mistresses were kept, bastards acknowledged. Many were brought home from France during the Revolution. Gentlemen considered lower-class women as their legitimate prey; they did not, generally, marry them. Respectable girls in search of husbands had to face competition from professionals and from willing amateurs among the poorer ranks.

'Women in low life', complained Mrs West, had *'slight ideas...of the value of chastity. Bastardy is scarcely reckoned a disgrace, and criminality before marriage is too common even to excite surprise.'* *'Criminality'* means sexual relations before the wedding; *'crim. con.'*, short for *'criminal conversation'*, was a slang phrase for unofficial intercourse.

Malthus explains why men waited so long to marry. The usual age seems to have been about thirty, as Emma observes.

> *A man of liberal education, but with an income only just sufficient to enable him to associate in the rank of gentlemen, must feel absolutely certain that if he marries and has a family he shall be obliged, if he mixes at all in society, to rank himself with moderate farmers and the lower class of tradesmen. The woman that a man of education would naturally make ... his choice would be one brought up in the same tastes and sentiments with himself and used to ... a society totally different from that to which she must be reduced by marriage.... Two or three steps of descent in society, particularly at this round of the ladder, where education ends and ignorance begins, will not be considered ... as a fancied and chimerical, but a real and essential evil.*

In other words, a man cannot ask a woman to marry him until he is in a position to keep her in the style to which she is accustomed.

Maria Edgeworth's novel *Patronage* defines *'pretty well married'* as to a man with an income of £2,000 a year; *'very well married'* meant over £10,000.

'Our sex is become too mercenary, and too dissipated, to feel an irresistible *penchant till they have obtained a side-glance at a swain's rent-roll'*, writes Mrs West, and Mary Wollstonecraft agrees:

> *Girls marry merely to better themselves...and have such*
> *perfect power over their hearts as not to permit themselves*
> *to fall in love till a man with a superior fortune offers.*

PRIDE AND PREJUDICE

This caution was, in the parlance of the day, *'prudence'*.
Elizabeth Bennet speaks for her generation when she asks: *'...*
what is the difference, in matrimonial affairs, between a mercenary
and a prudent motive? Where does discretion end, and avarice
begin?'[2]

Mr Bennet's property was

> *an estate of two thousand a year ... entailed on a distant*
> *relation. Their mother's fortune, though ample for her*
> *situation in life, could but ill supply the deficiency of his.*
> *Her father had been an attorney in Meryton, and had left*
> *her four thousand pounds.*[3]

Entails held estates together. By the legal process of entail the
succession to an estate could be controlled for generations. The
heir could not sell or mortgage except by Act of Parliament, an
expensive process. Wives usually brought dowries or 'portions'
with them, used to buy more land. Adam Smith noted: *'Entails*
are the natural consequence of the law of primogeniture.' He
thought it absurd that *'the property of the present generation should*
be restrained and regulated according to the fancy of those who died
perhaps 500 years ago'.

The entail, which Mrs Bennet resents without understanding,
causes the poverty of the Bennet girls. As their mother is bitterly
aware, Mr Collins, after Mr Bennet dies, will have the right, in
Mr Bennet's words, to *'turn you all out of this house as soon as he*
pleases'. Females could not inherit entailed property.

No wonder Mrs Bennet complains: *'I am sure I do not know*
who is to maintain you when your father is dead.'[4] No wonder she
has daydreams of a *'smart young colonel with five or six thousand a*
year'.[5]

Her daughters are handicapped socially as well as financially.
Mrs Hurst, sister of the eligible Mr Bingley, says Jane is a very
sweet girl, *'but with such a father and mother, and such low*
connections...'.[6] It is mentioned that their uncle is an attorney in

Meryton (an attorney was a lawyer inferior to a barrister); another *'lives somewhere near Cheapside'*. People of fashion did not live near Cheapside, the commercial eastern part of London, within the city.

Mr Bingley says this does not make the girls less agreeable, but Mr Darcy agrees that low relations must damage the girls' chances of marrying well.

Yet Mr Gardiner, who is in business in London, is *'a sensible, gentlemanlike man'* (high praise); Mrs Gardiner is *'an amiable, intelligent, elegant woman'*. Mr Darcy comes to recognize their worth.[7] Jane Austen is sharp about the snobbery of Mrs Hurst and her sister Miss Bingley: they *'would have had difficulty in believing that a man who lived by trade, and in view of his own warehouses, could have been so well-bred and agreeable'*.

Yet the Bingley fortune has been made in trade. The daughters are

> *proud and conceited ... had a fortune of twenty thousand pounds ... they were of a respectable family in the north of England, a circumstance more deeply impressed on their memories than that their brother's fortune and their own had been acquired in trade.*[8]

Mr Bingley's income of £5,000 a year comes from the £100,000 left by his father who had intended to purchase an estate, but did not live to do it. Sometimes Bingley thinks he might settle at Netherfield, which he is renting, and leave the next generation to buy, but his sisters are *'very anxious for his having an estate of his own'*.[9] Mrs Hurst, whose husband has style, but not too much money, likes to impose on her good-natured brother's hospitality.

Elizabeth recognizes that Mr Bingley's sisters look down on her family: *'We are not rich enough, or grand enough for them.'*[10]

Despite Jane's beauty and Elizabeth's wit, the Bennet girls are not eligible matches. On the lower fringes of the gentry, they have nothing to tempt suitors with. When Elizabeth asks her father to restrain Lydia's wildness lest she be taken advantage of, her father replies that Lydia is *'luckily too poor to be an object of prey to anybody'*.[11]

Mr Collins, heir to the estate, clumsily tries to make up for the injustice by offering to marry one of the girls. Hearing that Jane is likely to become engaged, he proposes to Elizabeth, in terms which are unconsciously insulting.

> '*To fortune I am perfectly indifferent, and shall make no
> demand of that nature on your father, since I am perfectly
> well aware that it could not be complied with; and that one
> thousand pounds in the four per cents which will not be
> yours till after your mother's decease is all that you may
> ever be entitled to . . .*'[12]

Mr Collins is not unusual in making these calculations; he is
merely tactless in mentioning them so bluntly to Elizabeth.
When she refuses him he tries to bring pressure on her by
pointing out the brutal realities:

> '*Your portion is unhappily so small that it will in all
> likelihood undo the effects of all your loveliness and amiable
> qualifications.*'[13]

Elizabeth, to her mother's annoyance, refuses Mr Collins, but
she knows the economic facts of life. '*Handsome young men must
have something to live on, as well as the plain*',[14] she says when the
attractive adventurer Wickham deserts her to court an heiress.
When it becomes necessary to persuade him to marry her sister
Lydia, she says: '*Wickham will never marry a woman without some
money. He cannot afford it.*'[15]

Her father lets Lydia have £50 a year, the income on her
inheritance of £1,000.

Darcy's cousin Fitzwilliam, the younger son of an earl, spells
out to Elizabeth that he cannot afford to be seriously interested
in her. She says:

> '*Younger sons cannot marry where they like. Unless where
> they like women of fortune, which I think they very often
> do.*'
>
> '*Our habits of expense make us too dependent, and there
> are not many in my rank of life who can afford to marry
> without some attention to money.*'[16]

Miss Darcy's fortune is £30,000, which explains why
Wickham tried to run away with her. Until the Married
Women's Property Act of 1870 a woman's property became her
husband's unless a separate 'settlement' was made upon her.
Each of Jane Austen's characters carries a price-tag, and
Elizabeth's is low.

Jane West warns young women '*from aiming at conquest, on the
score of their personal attractions, to which neither their birth,*

connexions, education, nor situation entitle them to aspire'. We are reminded that in Lady Catherine's view Elizabeth is a *'young woman without family, connections or fortune'*, and therefore her claim to Darcy is *'upstart pretension'*.[17]

For Elizabeth to catch Darcy, with his £10,000 a year, is indeed an amazingly good match, beyond her reasonable expectations. This was an income on a ducal scale. She goes from comparative poverty to vast riches.

Gisborne is satirical about the common interpretation of the expression, *'a good match'*. It means, he writes,

> *taking place of other ladies in the neighbourhood; of decking herself out in jewels and lace;...splendid apartments; rolling in handsome carriages ... in a degree higher than that which a calculating broker, after poring on her pedigree, summing up her property in hand, and computing, at the market price, ... would have pronounced her entitled.*

Jane Austen may have had this passage in mind when writing of Mrs Bennet's joy when Elizabeth announces she is engaged to Darcy:

> *'Oh!...how rich and great you will be. What pin-money, what jewels, what carriages you will have!...A house in town! Everything that is charming...'*[18]

Few girls could have such fairy-tale good luck. In the real world, people have to compromise, like Charlotte Lucas, who scoops up Mr Collins after Elizabeth has rejected him, *'solely from the pure and disinterested desire of an establishment'*.[19]

Charlotte's parents are delighted:

> *Mr Collins's present circumstances made it a most eligible match for their daughter, to whom they could give little fortune; and his prospects of future wealth were exceedingly fair.*[20]

When Elizabeth tactlessly reveals her astonishment at the news of the engagement, Charlotte says quietly: *'I am not romantic, you know. I never was. I ask only a comfortable home.'*[21] The glittering prizes are few and far between; most people have to settle for what they can get.

> *Mr Collins ... was neither sensible nor agreeable; his society was irksome ... but still he would be her husband.*

Mrs Bennet is, for once, 'unable to utter a syllable' on hearing that Elizabeth is engaged to Darcy. (*Pride and Prejudice* p. 378) (Illustration by Hugh Thomson for the 1911 Macmillan edition)

Mr Collins proposes to Charlotte who has waited in the lane. (*Pride and Prejudice* p. 121) (Illustrations by Hugh Thomson for the 1911 Macmillan edition)

> *Without thinking highly either of men or of matrimony,*
> *marriage had always been her object; it was the only*
> *honourable provision for well educated young women of*
> *small fortune, and however uncertain of giving happiness,*
> *must be their pleasantest preservative from want.*[22]

Charlotte knows such an opportunity does not come every day.
She is, after all, twenty-seven. She makes the best of things.
Charlotte is no fool. Jane Bennet is very much in love with
Bingley, but keeps her feelings under such control that Darcy
believes she is indifferent. Knowing Bingley is taken with her,
Darcy persuades him to move out of danger, causing Jane much
heartache. Charlotte is shrewdly aware of the problem:

> *It is sometimes a disadvantage to be so very guarded. If a*
> *woman conceals her affection ... from the object of it, she*
> *may lose the opportunity of fixing him.*[23]

There was no intermediate stage of intimacy between
friendship and an engagement. Young men and girls did not go
out alone together. It was thus difficult for either sex to know
whether the people they were attracted to felt the same way, or
whether their smiles were mere politeness. That is why people in
Jane Austen suffer so many misunderstandings, such anxieties as
to whether the people they love return their feelings.

Relations before marriage were formal and distant, so it was
difficult to find out a man's true character. The risks involved in
making a choice were considerable. The smooth deceivers, like
Wickham in *Pride and Prejudice*, Mr Elliot in *Persuasion*, were a
real, everyday danger. Divorce was possible only for the very
rich, by Act of Parliament. Although men could divorce
unfaithful wives, there was no provision for any wife, however
abused, to take proceedings against her husband.

'*It is a truth universally acknowledged, that a single man in*
possession of a good fortune, must be in want of a wife.' This
famous sentence opens *Pride and Prejudice*. Jane Austen was
using a current formula: Gisborne wrote: '*it is universally*
acknowledged that the intellectual powers of women are not
restricted to the arts of the housekeeper and sempstress'; Malthus
writes: '*It is an acknowledged truth in philosophy that a just theory*
will always be confirmed by experiment....'; Burke writes: '*It*
appears ... to be generally acknowledged, that with regard to truth
and falsehood there is something fixed ....'

Jane Austen is making a philosophical joke. It is the anxious mothers and daughters who '*universally acknowledge*' the need for a wife; the women in her society need husbands so urgently that their wishes fill their horizon and become, for them, '*acknowledged truth*'.

EMMA

As we have seen (Chapter 3), for unengaged girls to write to young men was a breach of the proprieties. Jane Fairfax and Frank Churchill are within their rights in keeping up a correspondence, since they are engaged. Jane goes to the post office every morning to fetch letters, and has to parry awkward questions.

But their secret engagement deeply hurts his father and stepmother. Marriage was not a private arrangement between individuals, but a public contract involving money and families. Jane Fairfax acknowledges that she has behaved badly, and that the secrecy has brought its own punishment. Frank, anxious for concealment, has flirted blatantly with Emma, and made Jane jealous.

Emma, too, feels it was not right for Frank to come among them, an engaged man, '*with manners so very disengaged*'. He and Jane have behaved in an underhand, unacceptable fashion.

Jane's jealousy is tied up with anxiety about her future. If Frank does not marry her, she faces the grim prospect of becoming a governess. Mrs Elton insists on trying to find her a job, unaware that Jane hopes to escape by marriage. Jane politely refuses Mrs Elton's officious offers, saying:

> '*There are places in town, offices, where inquiry would soon produce something.—Offices for the sale—not quite of human flesh—but of human intellect.*'
> '*Oh! my dear, human flesh! You quite shock me; if you mean a fling at the slave trade . . .*' [Mrs Elton is perhaps a little touchy on this point.]
> '*I did not mean, I was not thinking, of the slave trade,*' replied Jane; '*governess-trade, I assure you, was all that I had in view; widely different certainly as to the guilt of those who carry it on; but as to the greater misery of the victims, I do not know where it lies.*'[24]

We may think Jane is making a disproportionate fuss about having to get a job, but being a governess was a lonely, humiliating existence. Governesses were too refined to mix comfortably with the servants, but were kept at a distance by the families who employed them.

Mary Wollstonecraft wrote:

> *The few employments open to women, so far from being liberal, are menial, and when a superior education enables them to take charge of the education of children as governesses, they are not treated like the tutors of sons . . . .*

Mary Wollstonecraft wrote from painful experience; she had been governess in Ireland to the children of the Countess of Kingston, and had quarrelled bitterly with her employer.

Mr Knightley is glad that Miss Taylor has married Mr Weston and that she is sure of a comfortable provision. Emma, insulated by wealth, is less sensitive. She, young and rich as she is, says gaily:

> *'It is poverty only which makes celibacy contemptible . . . a single woman, with a very narrow income, must be a ridiculous, disagreeable old maid.'*[25]

The poverty of Miss Bates, living with her aged mother in a couple of rooms *'on the drawing room floor'* of somebody else's house, with one servant and no oven of their own, is contrasted with Emma's affluence. Mr Knightley says of Miss Bates:

> *'She is poor; she has sunk from the comforts she was born to; and, if she live to old age, must probably sink more.'*[26]

'Single women have a dreadful propensity for being poor—which is one very strong argument in favour of matrimony', wrote Jane Austen to her niece, Fanny Knight, on 13th March 1817. Jane was at that time forty-two, unmarried herself, and far from well-off.

Mary Wollstonecraft urged that women should be trained for real professions; they might become physicians instead of home nurses, for example. Jane West sharply takes her to task: women must accept their *'dependent state and circumscribed abilities'*. However, she insists on prudence, if not independence: *'. . . single women must be economical and have a knowledge of business and money transactions not to be imposed upon'*. They should be *'as useful to others as their limited means allow'*, respectable and happy. This is the lifestyle accepted by Miss Bates, and possibly by Jane Austen.

PERSUASION

Anne Elliot is twenty-seven, still single after being persuaded by Lady Russell that it would be foolish and reckless to marry Captain Wentworth. She is advised to wait till somebody more eligible, who can offer security, comes along. In her loneliness, however, Anne eventually comes to regret her decision since she finds that her life, with its routines of charitable visiting and family peacemaking, is petty and uneventful. She needs strict self-discipline if she is not to fall into depression and self-pity.

Her sister Elizabeth, also unmarried, still older, is even less content than Anne. Elizabeth has '*no habits of utility abroad, nor talents or accomplishments for home*'. Her life is one of '*sameness and ... elegance, ... prosperity and ... nothingness ... a long uneventful residence in one country circle*'.[27]

> *Men have various employments and pursuits which engage their attention, and give a character to the opening mind*, wrote Mary Wollstonecraft, with her usual forceful skill in isolating the issue, *but women, confined to one, and having their thoughts constantly directed to the most insignificant part of themselves, seldom extend their views beyond the triumph of the hour.*

Anne Elliot, talking of women's constancy in love compared with men's, says to Captain Harville:

> '*We certainly do not forget you, so soon as you forget us ... We live at home, quiet, confined, and our feelings prey on us. You are forced on exertion. You have always a profession, pursuits, business of some sort or other ...*'[28]

In Anne's case, '*no second attachment ... had been possible to ... the fastidiousness of her taste, in the small limits of the society around them*'.[29] The criteria for a husband, said Lady Sarah Pennington, were virtue and good nature, preferably with understanding (intelligence). Sidney Smith advised a young girl: '*Don't marry any body who has not a tolerable understanding and a thousand a year, and God bless you, dear child.*'

This was common sense, or prudence. Mary Wollstonecraft observed that '*women are so often degraded by suffering the selfish prudence of age to chill the ardour of youth*'. The problem is dramatized in the story of Anne Elliot.

'We live at home, quiet, confined, and our feelings prey on us.' This picture, by John Constable, *Girl posing at a window*, shows a young woman looking out on the world from inside, like Jane Austen's heroines. (Courtauld Institute)

> *She had been forced into prudence in her youth, she learned romance as she grew older—the natural sequel of an unnatural beginning.*[30]

'*Nothing can compare to the misery of being bound without love*', wrote Jane Austen to Fanny Knight on 30th November 1814. Contemporaries agreed with her (though the economic system meant that loveless marriages were made every day). Mary Wollstonecraft employed the term '*legal prostitution*' for a loveless, mercenary marriage. Moralists agreed that if one could not marry for love, then '*esteem*' or respect was the next best thing. There could be no happiness without it. Earlier in the eighteenth century, daughters had been disposed of, without their consent. Now, parents no longer forced their daughters, but they could and did apply moral pressure. It was important to choose a man of principle, not one whose '*vices*' in the words of Jane West, '*will either corrupt our principles or wring our hearts with the most poignant misery*'. Lady Sarah Pennington advised her absent daughters to choose a man of '*really virtuous principle—an unaffected goodness of heart*'.

'*Wisdom is better than wit*', Jane Austen advised Fanny Knight, on 18th November 1814. '*...Anything is to be preferred or endured rather than marrying without affection.*' Three years later, she wrote to the same niece: '*Think of his father's objection, of want of money...of sheets sewn across...*'. Fear of poverty was real, but did not justify ambitious and mercenary marriage.

The view of married life in Jane Austen's letters is detached and unromantic. To Fanny Knight, 20th February 1817, she writes: '*I shall hate you when your delicious play of mind is all settled down into conjugal and maternal affections.*' She had just viewed a new baby: '*I would recommend to her and Mr D. the simple regimen of separate rooms.*'

Children came frequently: she wrote to Fanny on 13th March: '*Anna has had a bad cold, looks pale, and we fear something else. She has just weaned Julia.*' She advises Fanny:

> *Do not be in a hurry; ... the right man will come at last ... by not beginning the business of mothering quite so early in life, you will be young in constitution, spirits, figure and countenance, while Mrs William Hammond is growing old by confinements and nursing.*

There was no birth control to speak of. On 8th February 1807, Jane wrote to Cassandra: '*...that Mrs Deedes is to have another child I suppose I may lament*'. In the same letter she observes:

> *Miss Jackson is married to young Mr Gunthorpe, and is to be very unhappy. He swears, drinks, is cross, jealous, selfish and brutal; the match makes* her *family miserable, and has occasioned* his *being disinherited.*

[1] W. H. Auden, Letter to Lord Byron, Part 1 *Letters from Iceland* (Faber, 1937) p. 21   [2] Jane Austen *Pride and Prejudice* p. 153   [3] *ibid.* p. 28   [4] *ibid.* p. 113   [5] *ibid.* p. 29   [6] *ibid.* p. 36   [7] *ibid.* p. 255   [8] *ibid.* p. 15   [9] *ibid.* p. 15   [10] *ibid.* p. 119   [11] *ibid.* p. 232   [12] *ibid.* p. 106   [13] *ibid.* p. 108   [14] *ibid.* p. 150   [15] *ibid.* p. 283   [16] *ibid.* p. 183   [17] *ibid.* p. 356   [18] *ibid.* p. 378   [19] *ibid.* p. 122   [20] *ibid.* p. 122   [21] *ibid.* p. 125   [22] *ibid.* p. 122   [23] *ibid.* p. 21   [24] Jane Austen *Emma* p. 300   [25] *ibid.* p. 85   [26] *ibid.* p. 375   [27] Jane Austen *Persuasion* p. 9   [28] *ibid.* p. 233   [29] *ibid.* p. 28   [30] *ibid.* p. 30

6

Culture and education

During the War, which lasted till the peace of Waterloo in 1815, the Grand Tour of Europe on which young men travelled with their tutors was no longer possible. There were a few months of peace in 1802, when a few young men set off, but they found themselves trapped when fighting started again. The poet Byron, unable to cross the Alps to Italy, skirted the battle zone by a southerly route, through Spain and Italy to Greece and Turkey.

The Grand Tour developed the taste of the young men who took it, though some benefited more than others. Sir Joshua Reynolds (who founded the Royal Academy in 1786) once saw some Englishmen in the Vatican gallery, probably the world's greatest collection of Italian primitive religious paintings. They spent hours, reported Sir Joshua, writing notes dictated to them by their guide. *'They scarcely ever looked at the paintings the whole time.'*

PRIDE AND PREJUDICE

Jane Austen went to the Society of Painters exhibition in Spring Gardens, and wrote to Cassandra on 24th May 1813:

> *It is not thought a good collection, but I was very well pleased—particularly ... with a small portrait of Mrs Bingley, excessively like her. I went in hopes of seeing one of her sister, but there was no Mrs Darcy ... I have no chance of her in the collection of Sir Joshua Reynolds's paintings which is now showing in Pall Mall ...*

We would give a great deal now to know which paintings could reflect Jane Austen's own ideas of Jane and Elizabeth Bennet.

Mr Collins reads Dr Fordyce's sermons aloud to the Bennet girls. Lydia interrupts the reading with yawns of boredom. In the sermons, Fordyce distinguishes between the *'noisy, empty, trivial chatter of everlasting folly'* which *'it is too much for human patience to sustain'* and *'the playful spirit in conversation ... which, blended with good sense, and kept within reasonable bounds, contributes, like the lighter and more careless touches in a picture, to give an air of ease and freedom'.*

This contrast may have been in Jane Austen's mind when she created the talk of *'thoughtless Lydia'* and her playful sister Elizabeth, who demonstrates good sense.

Mr Collins, invited to read aloud to the ladies, is offered a novel, but insists he never reads them. *'After some deliberation he chose Fordyce's sermons.'*[1] Dr Fordyce is uncompromisingly against novels. In his sermons we read:

> *We consider the general run of novels is utterly unfit for you. Instruction they convey none. They paint scenes of pleasure and passion altogether improper for you to behold, even with the mind's eye.... She who can bear to peruse them must in her soul be a prostitute.*

We are now in a position to grasp the subtlety of Jane Austen's allusive joke about sermons and novel-reading, in the course of a novel, the form Fordyce considered *'shameful'* and *'pestiferous'*.

Gisborne attacked *'the mischievous trash which the circulating library pours forth for the entertainment of a mind unaccustomed to reflection'.* The circulating library was available to those who could pay a small subscription.

We grow up with the idea that the novel is a vehicle for serious moral discussion, but in Jane Austen's time only poetry, history and *belles lettres* and (especially) sermons, qualified as worthwhile reading. The fury and moral outrage with which novel-reading was attacked is hard for us to grasp.

Arthur Young's diary for 22nd May 1804, says:

> *Somebody called on Mrs Pelham and found her lying on a sofa reading a novel, rouged as much as any Madame la Marquise. They thought she seemed to be too high-flown to be asked to a sober party of whist. What a gradation of evil amongst the worldly even in the* respectable (soi-disant) *classes.*

On 10th January 1810, he found out, to his horror, that he had read a novel by mistake, believing it to be history.

It has unhinged me, and broken my attention to better things, which shows strongly how pernicious this sort of reading is, and what a powerful temptation to vice....Oh! the number of miserables that novels have sent to perdition.

This is not the calm, reasonable tone of the early eighteenth century, nor the robust one of the profligate Regency. It is the voice of the Evangelical religious reformers who were to create the moral climate of Queen Victoria's England. It is not surprising that Victoria, as a girl, was not allowed to read novels.

Even Samuel Taylor Coleridge (1772–1834), the romantic poet, wrote:

Where the reading of novels prevails as a habit, it occasions in time the entire destruction of the powers of the mind ; it is such an utter loss to the reader, that it is not so much to be called pass-time as kill-time.

The novelist Maria Edgeworth, contemporary with Jane Austen, thought novels encouraged '*folly, error and vice*'. She called her own novels '*moral tales*'.

Mrs Chapone's popular *Letters on the Improvement of the Mind* (1772) says novels are dangerous, because they '*inflame the passions of youth, whilst the chief purpose of education should be to moderate and restrain them*'. Mrs Chapone started her own literary career with a '*romance*', but chose to forget this.

Novels were read mainly by women. Anything which inflamed their passions was suspicious. Chastity, said Dr Johnson, was the first principle women were taught. Once that went, there was no hope of any other morality being maintained. This was widely believed. In practice, virginity was valued because it was the chief bargaining weapon the middle-class girl had in the marriage market. Chief among the readers of novels were middle-class girls.

The Romantic movement, well under way in Jane Austen's time, was fermenting from the 1730s onwards, as people felt the need for complex experiences, deeper emotions. They drifted eventually towards recognition of the cruelty in man which found expression in the events of the French Revolution and the writings of the Marquis de Sade.

But in mid-century, when the sentimental novel flourished, people liked to believe with Jean-Jacques Rousseau (1712–78) that man was naturally good, kindly and innocent. Society, laws and civilization were to blame for corrupting him. Man, if left alone by social institutions, would be wise, happy and good. The only problem seemed to be that of constructing an educational and social system which would free him to be so.

This was a controversial, although a popular, view, because it contradicted orthodox Christian teaching that man was born in a state of original sin and could only be saved by the grace of God. But for a while orthodox religion lost its hold and the cult of 'sensibility' or 'sentimentality' filled the vacuum. 'Sentimental' novels varied in quality, but all were intended to wring tears from the reader, and readers enjoyed having tears wrung from them. People were proud of their susceptibility to emotion.

People enjoyed crying: there is a yearning for the ambivalent attractions of pain, acknowledged above, in Laurence Sterne's books. Sophia, in Henry Fielding's *Tom Jones* (1749), *'loved a tender sensation'*.

NORTHANGER ABBEY

Although Samuel Richardson was a fervent Christian, his novel *Pamela or Virtue Rewarded* (1740) is often counted among the sentimental novels. Pamela is a servant girl whose master tries to seduce her, fails and finally marries her. Oliver Goldsmith's *The Vicar of Wakefield* (1776), a tragicomedy of clerical life, is considered *'sentimental'*, and so is Henry Mackenzie's *The Man of Feeling* (1771). There were hundreds of others, now forgotten. The heroes and heroines were extraordinary people, as we can work out from reading *Northanger Abbey*. They were beautiful, brilliant, talented, morally perfect and improbably blessed by fortune. It is this tendency in the popular novels of her day Jane Austen is mocking when she stresses Catherine Morland's ordinariness. The mockery is an expression of Jane Austen's distrust of cheap emotion and slack morals. The young woman who took her notions from fiction was a standard target for satire. Jane Austen enjoyed Charlotte Lennox's *The Female Quixote* which, like *Northanger Abbey*, made fun of such fictions. There were several novels which parodied the novelistic conventions in a similar way. Jane Austen started her writing career, in her teens, as a parodist.

The atmosphere of the Gothic novel, with its cobwebbed castles, survives in Hammer Horror films. Mrs Ann Radcliffe, author of *The Mysteries of Udolpho* (1794), wrote about gallant and virtuous heroes, innocent heroines, black-hearted villains, skeletons and black veils, set in haunted abbeys and castles in wild, forested mountain country. It is Mrs Radcliffe's books which fascinate and thrill Catherine and Isabella. All the books mentioned in *Northanger Abbey* are real ones. Heather Coombs writes in *The Age of Keats and Shelley*:

> *Mrs Radcliffe makes use of all the horrors of the supernatural, without supernatural events actually occurring. In* The Mysteries of Udolpho, *for example, Dorothée, the housekeeper, indicates the bed in which her mistress died, and which is now covered by a black counterpane:*

She had scarcely uttered these words, when the pall was more violently agitated than before; but Emily, somewhat ashamed of her terrors, stepped back to the bed, willing to be convinced that the wind only had occasioned her alarm; when, as she gazed within the curtains, the pall moved again, and, in the next moment, the apparition of a human countenance rose above it. Screaming with terror, they both fled.

> *It is something of an anticlimax when we discover later that it was no apparition, but a* real *human countenance, that of a smuggler, concealed in the bed.*
>
> *Similarly, the ghastly sight behind the black veil with which Mrs Radcliffe so delightfully terrorized poor Catherine in Jane Austen's* Northanger Abbey:

'I know it must be a skeleton; I am sure it is Laurentina's skeleton' —

> *turns out, tamely, to be a wax image made as a* 'memento mori'.
>
> *Nevertheless, there is nothing lame or disappointing about the settings of the novels. The castles are as medieval as the sternest critic could require:*

The towers were united by a curtain, pierced and embattled also, below which appeared the pointed arch of an huge portcullis —

> *and as ruined and gloomy as one could wish for:*

Emily...looked fearfully on the almost roofless walls green with damps, and on the gothic points of the windows, where the ivy and the briony had long supplied the place of glass, and ran mantling among the broken capitals of some columns, that had once supported the roof. Barnardine stumbled ... and his voice, as he uttered a sudden oath, was returned in hollow echoes.

Nor are the sufferings of heroes and heroines in Gothic novels allowed to be slight. Imprisonment, rape, murder — often at the hands of perverted nuns or monks — such things are commonplace, especially in the novel by Matthew Gregory Lewis, immensely popular and widely condemned when published in 1796, which earned him his nickname 'Monk' Lewis.

Such novels might well be regarded today as sheer escapism. On the surface, they appear to have little to do with realism — though a closer reading often reveals perceptive description of scenery and a real attempt to portray shifts of feeling. Certainly they appeared to Jane Austen to be totally divorced from reality, and for that reason their immense popularity was suspect. The ludicrous scene in Northanger Abbey, *in which Catherine struggles in the dark to discover the mysteries concealed in a black cabinet, only to find a laundry-bill, and the even more ludicrous suspicions she harbours concerning General Tilney's treatment of his wife, are grim warnings to young ladies too easily taken in by pleasures of the circulating libraries and it is the public taste which is being queried when Henry gently rebukes Catherine:*

'Consult your own understanding, your own sense of the probable, your own observation of what is passing around you ... what ideas have you been admitting?'[2]

Mrs Coombs's excellent chapter should be read in full.

On one level, *Northanger Abbey* is about the distinction between romance and reality; on another, the difference between rubbish novels and fiction with some roots in reality. We are now in a position to grasp Jane Austen's spirited defence of her craft:

If the heroine of one novel be not patronised by the heroine of another, from whom can she expect protection and regard.... Let us not desert one another; we are an injured body. Although our productions have afforded more extensive and unaffected pleasure than those of any other literary corporation in the world, no species of composition has been so much decried.... 'Oh! it is only a novel,' replies the young lady.... 'It is only Cecilia, *or* Camilla, *or* Belinda' *or in short, only some work in which the greatest powers of the mind are displayed, in which the most thorough knowledge of human nature, the happiest de-lineation of its varieties, the liveliest effusions of wit and humour are conveyed to the world in the best chosen language.*[3]

Cecilia and *Camilla* are novels by Fanny Burney; *Belinda* was by Maria Edgeworth. John Thorpe's contempt for Fanny Burney and her works because she married an emigrant, (M. D'Arblay), shows him to be a fool.[4] After Jane Austen's death, her brother Henry hoped her works might be judged fit to stand on the same shelf as those of '*a D'Arblay or an Edgeworth*'.

Mary Wollstonecraft (who, like Mrs West and the others, wrote novels herself) complained, with more justice than other opponents of the novel, that reading them made women '*very fond of using strong expressions and superlatives in conversation*'.

Lord Chesterfield attacks such affectations as '*vastly angry, vastly kind*', along with proverbs and '*vulgar aphorisms*' on 27th September 1749. Jane Austen wrote to Martha Lloyd on 29th November 1812:

> *Mary Deedes I think must be liked ... she is so perfectly unaffected and sweet tempered, and though as ready to be pleased as Fanny Cage, deals less in superlatives and rapture.*

Superlatives are used unthinkingly only by Jane Austen's sillier characters. Isabella Thorpe speaks of '*the prettiest hat you can imagine*'.[5] She surpasses herself by saying: '*The smallest income in nature would be enough for me.*'[6] Her imagination is nourished on cheap fiction.

Henry Tilney seems to agree that such reading does not tend to improve the speech of its readers. He mocks the indiscriminate usage of Catherine, when she asks him whether he does not think *Udolpho* '*the nicest book in the world?*'[7]

Henry replies that the word '*nice*' is overused. His sister Eleanor changes the subject, and asks Catherine if she is fond of '*that kind of reading*'.

Catherine replies that she doesn't much like any other.

> '... I can read poetry and plays, and things of that sort, and do
> not dislike travels, but history ... I cannot be interested in. Can
> you?'[8]

Eleanor intelligently defends the reading of history. The whole
passage is worth looking up. Jane Austen's brother Henry tells
us:

> Her reading was very extensive in history and belles lettres
> ...her favourite moral writers were Johnson in prose and
> Cowper in verse.

Locke said it was good to be well-read in modern history, and
Eleanor Tilney clearly speaks for the cultivated opinion of her
time. Jane Austen envied her brother Francis the chance to go to
Sweden (31st July 1813):

> ... the country of Gustavus-Vasa, and Charles 12th. and
> Christina, and Linnaeus—do their ghosts rise up before
> you? I have a great respect for former Sweden. So zealous
> as it was for Protestantism!

Yet it is clear from *Northanger Abbey* that while they could
read history, women were not expected to discuss politics. '*From
politics, it was a short step to silence.*'[9]
Gisborne urges the need

> to call forth the reasoning powers of girls ... and to enrich
> the mind with useful and interesting knowledge suitable to
> their sex. The foundation is laid by communicating to the
> scholar a rational insight into the formation and idioms of
> her native tongue. She will thus avoid the grammatical
> blunders which used to disgrace the conversation even of
> women in the upper and middle ranks of life, and in
> conjunction with erroneous orthography [spelling] to
> deform their epistolary correspondence, that in some years
> hence it may perhaps no longer be easy to find a young lady
> who professes to be mistress of the French language, and is
> at the same time grossly ignorant of her own. Geography,
> select parts of natural history, or of the history of different
> nations, ancient or modern, popular and amusing facts in
> astronomy and in other sciences, are often familiar to the
> daughter in a degree which, at the very moment that it

delights the parent, reminds her how small a portion of such information was in her youth imparted to herself.

There is ample evidence that women were speaking and writing more acceptably. People who cannot spell, or are ignorant of geography, are laughed at in Jane Austen's novels. Catherine Morland has no idea of her route from Gloucestershire back to Wiltshire, except that she will pass the spire of Salisbury.[10]

Her education has been sketchy, but probably typical:

> *Writing and accounts she was taught by her father; French by her mother ... and shirked her lessons ... whenever she could.*[11]

The heroines of fiction such as Catherine enjoys are all skilful musicians without effort. Catherine, more like the small girls we know, learned music for a year, because her mother wanted her to, but *'could not bear it'*. She had expected to like it, *'had been fond of tinkling the keys of the old forlorn spinet'*.[12]

The spinet was neglected because the pianoforte was the now fashionable instrument. Although all *'accomplished'* girls were supposed to play and sing, Jane Austen shows how forced such interest must often have been. Her women do not always keep up their music after marriage, although they have few household duties.

The education of women was a controversial issue and the picture more complicated than is commonly believed.

Lord Chesterfield mentions a woman who, *'though she understands Latin perfectly well, ... wisely conceals it'*. (22nd October 1750) When Lismahago, in *Humphry Clinker*, makes a Latin quotation at dinner, he has to explain it, *'in deference to the ladies'*. Intelligent girls were not taught Latin and Greek, but were encouraged to study modern languages, history, geography and music. Jane Austen read French easily and knew some Italian, according to her brother's account.

'We are educated in the grossest ignorance', wrote Lady Mary Wortley-Montagu on 10th October 1752, *'... our knowledge must rest concealed, and be as useless to the world as gold in the mine'*. On 28th January 1753, she warns that her grand-daughter must learn *'to conceal whatever learning she attains'*.

Dr Gregory's *Legacy to his Daughters* (1774) enjoined, *'if you have any learning, keep it a profound secret, especially from the*

men...'. Fordyce the sermon-writer agreed: '*Wit...is especially...
dreaded in women.*'

Gisborne, to his credit, probed this conventional wisdom:

> *Men, it is said, are not partial to women of strong
> understandings.... Because a man is absurd, is a woman to
> be a hypocrite?*

Mary Mitford wrote in 1812:

> *In this educating age everything is taught to women except
> that which is perhaps worth all the rest—the power and
> habit of thinking.*

Everybody, including Lady Mary Wortley-Montagu and Dr Johnson, agreed
that a woman ought to be skilful with her needle. There were no sewing-
machines and sheets had to be hemmed by hand. In Jane Austen's bedroom at
Chawton we see the patchwork quilt she made with her mother and sister in
blues, rusty browns and cream colours. (J. Butler-Kearney)

Mary Wollstonecraft argued that women might study for business and the professions. Jane West attacked her as '...*an eccentric writer, who mistook insubordination for independence of soul....My conviction is that we should make wretched generals, patriots, politicians, legislators and advocates ... the warmth of our hearts overpowers ... our judgement.*' Mrs West has no wish to see the '*female world ... abound with metaphysicians, historians, speculative philosophers, or learned ladies of any kind*'.

It is against the background of such opinions that we must consider Jane Austen's famous comment:

> *A woman especially, if she have the misfortune of knowing anything, should conceal it as well as she can.*[13]

We are apt to think that the contemptuous and satirical attitude to '*accomplishment*' is modern, but it was much in evidence in the eighteenth century.

Fordyce writes in the 1760s:

> *Parents ... down to the lowest tradesman, or mechanic, who to ape his superiors strains himself ... send their daughters to boarding schools ... they learn chiefly, to dress, to dance, to speak bad French, to prattle much nonsense....*

Jane West, fifty years later, says the manners of the age '*attach undue pre-eminence to exterior graces and accomplishments ... French, drawing, dancing, skill in dress ... so sedulously inculcated in the daughters of inferior tradesmen, yeomen and mechanics*' gave a '*meretricious rather than an engaging appearance*'.

Much of the outcry against mere '*accomplishment*' was a complaint that the daughters of social inferiors were getting above themselves. Without the background, intellectual and moral, given by aristocratic culture, it was implied, their warblings, tinklings and chatter could be based only on unsure foundations. The culture of our own daughters, to be sure, was the real thing.

Gisborne writes:

> *Far too great regard is usually paid to showy and superficial accomplishments....Fathers and mothers fix the thoughts of their children principally upon them; and thus excite and strengthen those passions which it ought to be an object of daily care to subdue.*

MANSFIELD PARK

Jane Austen had read Hannah More's *Coelebs in Search of a Wife* (1809). Charles Coeleb's view of the matter is as follows:

> *I call education, not that which smothers a woman with accomplishments, but that which tends to consolidate a firm and regular system of character ... not that which is made up of the shreds and patches of useless arts, but that which inculcates principles, polishes taste, regulates temper, cultivates reason, subdues the passions, directs the feelings, habituates to reflection, trains to self-denial and, most especially, that which refers all actions, feelings, sentiments, tastes and passions to the love and fear of God.*

Jane Austen shared these values: they underlie her picture of the Bertram girls in *Mansfield Park*. Their education is more superficial, and leads to disaster.

Culture of the mind, for eighteenth-century moralists, meant cultivation of the habits of reflection and self-discipline in order that the passions should be subdued by reason. Locke wrote that *'virtue ... is the hard and valuable part to be aimed at in education. ... All other considerations and accomplishments should give way. ...'*

Lady Mary Wortley-Montagu (28th January 1753) agreed:

> *The use of knowledge in our sex, beside the amusement of solitude, is to moderate the passions, and learn to be contented with a small expense, which are the certain effects of a studious life.*

For Gisborne, education meant learning *'the principles of conduct'*. He also recommended that poetry should be learned by heart, particularly Milton, Thompson, Gray, Mason and Cowper (a predictable eighteenth-century list). Jane Austen took the name of Fanny Price, heroine of *Mansfield Park*, from Crabbe's poem, 'The Parish Register' (1807). Crabbe's Fanny Price, like Jane Austen's, refused a rich admirer and remained true to her first love. Wordsworth wrote of Crabbe that *'nineteen or twenty of Crabbe's pictures are mere matters of fact'*, like *'medical reports'* or *'law cases'*. But Jane Austen liked him: she wrote to Cassandra (6th November 1813): *'Miss Lee I found very conversible; she admires Crabbe as she ought.'* In the novel, Fanny Price's own collection of books includes Crabbe's *Tales* and Dr Johnson's *The Idler*.

Mansfield Park has a library, unlike *nouveau riche* houses ('*Your hasty wealth thinks not of that*', said John Byng): with all its faults, Mansfield is a place where *Quarterly Reviews*[14] and other literary periodicals are lying around. Its cultural opportunities are wasted by the eldest son, Tom, a gambler, whose losses on the horses at Newmarket mean that the family living at Mansfield, which was being kept for Edmund, has to be sold to Dr Grant. The girls are vain and shallow, amazed at their cousin's ignorance when she arrives. They boast of their knowledge of

> '*the kings of England, with the dates of their accession, and most of the principal events of their reigns . . . the Roman emperors as low as Severus . . . heathen mythology . . . metals, semi-metals, planets and distinguished philosophers.*'[15]

This is merely what Locke calls '*learned rubbish*'. As the omniscient narrator tells us, Maria and Julia are '*entirely deficient in the less common acquirements of self-knowledge, generosity and humility. In everything but disposition, they were admirably taught*'.[16]

Fanny takes all the opportunities of cultural development Mansfield offers her. Staying in her Portsmouth home, and seeing its intellectual deprivation, she takes Susan's education in hand. She and Susan sit upstairs, at first '*only working*' (sewing) '*and talking*', but soon Fanny joins a circulating library. Although in Susan '*the early habit of reading was wanting*',[17] the girls read essays and history. Fanny, reared in a more propitious environment, has been a collector of books '*from the first hour of her commanding a shilling*'. She is passing on her intellectual wealth to her sister.

Fanny does not like Henry Crawford, recognizing that he thinks '*slightly . . . carelessly . . . unfeelingly*',[18] but when he reads Shakespeare, she is forced to listen. '*His reading was capital, and her pleasure in good reading extreme.*'[19] Reading aloud was a common way of passing the evening. The journals and diaries of the Shelley circle record '*reading together*'.

The Crawfords are pleasant, well-informed and amusing. Yet Mary gives herself away with everything she says, showing herself mercenary and self-centred (though she is kind to Fanny).

Mary refuses to form her own conclusions, preferring prejudices and 'hunches'. Quarrelling with Edmund about how far they have walked, she refuses to be *'dictated to by a watch ... she would not calculate, she would not compare'.*[20] She might have done better to take the advice of Jane West: *The science of numbers may ... be resorted to ... as a preservative from credulity.*

Edmund alone among the Bertram children seems undamaged by the mistakes made by his parents. Locke warns against alienating children by *'a constant stiffness, and a mien of authority and distance'.* This is certainly the manner Sir Thomas maintains with his children, and he is ultimately disappointed when he finds out that he does not know their true characters. As for his wife, *'to the education of her daughters Lady Bertram paid not the smallest attention'.*[21]

With a father outwardly severe and unapproachable, a mother utterly neglectful, it is not surprising that three of the four children turn out badly. Eventually Sir Thomas comes to realize that the education he gave his children was inadequate:

> *He feared that principle, active principle, had been wanting, that they had never been properly taught to govern their inclinations and tempers, by that sense of duty which can alone suffice. They had been instructed theoretically in their religion, but never required to bring it into daily practice. To be distinguished for elegance and accomplishments—the authorised object of their youth—could have had no useful influence that way, no moral effect on the mind. He had meant them to be good, but his cares had been directed to the understanding and manners, not the disposition; and of the necessity of self-denial and humility, he feared they had never heard from any lips that could profit them.*[22]

There is no room for doubt about the positive values Jane Austen believed in where education was concerned.

[1] Jane Austen *Pride and Prejudice* p. 28   [2] Heather Coombs *The Age of Keats and Shelley* (Blackie, 1978) pp. 101–3   [3] Jane Austen *Northanger Abbey* pp. 37–8   [4] *ibid.* p. 49   [5] *ibid.* p. 39   [6] *ibid.* p. 119   [7] *ibid.* p. 107   [8] *ibid.* p. 108   [9] *ibid.* p. 111   [10] *ibid.* p. 232   [11] *ibid.* p. 14   [12] *ibid.* p. 14   [13] *ibid.* p. 110   [14] Jane Austen *Mansfield Park* p. 104   [15] *ibid.* pp. 18–19   [16] *ibid.* p. 19   [17] *ibid.* p. 419   [18] *ibid.* p. 306   [19] *ibid.* p. 337   [20] *ibid.* p. 96   [21] *ibid.* p. 19   [22] *ibid.* p. 463

7

The professions and services

The professions recruited mainly from among the well-born younger sons, though some professions were considered gentlemanly and some were not. (See Chapter 2.) Young men of good family were likely to go in for the law, the Church or the armed services.

The functions of government were narrower than today. It took no responsibility for education or public health, and there was no welfare or social security, except for *'parish relief'*. The parish was the unit of administration, so the quality of its leadership, and of the professional men who served it, was crucial. This is an important theme in *Emma* and in *Mansfield Park*. Until the Parliamentary Reform Bill of 1832, neither Manchester nor Birmingham was represented in Parliament. The right to vote was limited to householders in certain towns and small landowners (the people Jane Austen writes about) in the country. Mary Wollstonecraft was way ahead of her time in 1792:

> *I may excite laughter, by dropping an hint, which I mean to pursue ... for I really think that women ought to have representatives, instead of being arbitrarily governed.*

EMMA

Mr John Knightley, the younger son and not the inheritor of Donwell, has of necessity to choose a profession. He is a successful barrister, with a London practice. He is *'gentlemanlike, and very clever ... but with reserved manners which prevented his being generally pleasing'*. But although his character lacks charm, he passes the test of integrity. He is *'respectable in his private character'*.[1]

The increase in population and prosperity during the eighteenth century was matched by expansion in the professions of the law, medicine and the clergy.

The word '*doctor*' was rarely used, except for doctors of divinity. Physicians were members of the Royal College of Physicians, founded by Henry VIII. They were gentlemen by birth and education. Most people were attended by the humbler apothecaries, whose fees were lower. Gisborne said physicians were

> *almost invariably men of liberal education and cultivated minds ... the art of medicine is carried among us to a singular height of excellence.... It opens the way to reputation and wealth, and raises the physician to a level, in the intercourse of common life, with the highest classes of society.*

He suggests that the charitable physician should treat deserving cases for nothing.

This would have encroached, in fact, on the livelihood of the apothecaries, who treated patients, although their main function was to supply medicines. Jane Austen's characters are usually attended by apothecaries, and occasionally by surgeons. Apothecaries were apprenticed as boys, the sons of prosperous farmers, tradesmen and sometimes of gentlemen who had come down in the world. Some apothecaries did well for themselves.

Parson Woodforde wrote in his diary for 15th July 1784: '*Mr Rand is a man of very good fortune, keeps a carriage and is an apothecary and has great business*'.

Mr Perry, the apothecary in *Emma*, prospers and makes enough money to set up his carriage like the gentry. Like other characters in *Emma*, Mr Perry is self-made. The author describes him as an '*intelligent, gentlemanlike man*'.

However, medical men could not presume too far. On 10th August 1814, Jane Austen wrote to her niece Anna Austen who had sent her the manuscript of a novel:

> *I have also scratched out the introduction between Lord P and his brother and Mr Griffin. A country surgeon (don't tell Mr C. Lyford) would not be introduced to men of their rank.*

By our standards, medicine had reached no great '*heights of excellence*'. Jane wrote to Cassandra, on 7th January 1808:

> *Two or three things I recollected ... one is, that the Welbys have lost their eldest son by a putrid fever at Eton, and another that Tom Chute is going to settle in Norfolk.*

'*Putrid*' sore throats and fevers frequently carried people off. Innoculation early in the eighteenth century, vaccination later, controlled smallpox, but measles was often fatal. People were realizing, however, that cleanliness was important for health.

Gilbert White wrote:

> ...*a leper is now a rare sight ... this happy change, perhaps, may have originated and been continued from the much smaller quantity of salted meat and fish now eaten ... from the use of linen next the skin; ...better bread; and ... the profusion of fruits, roots, légumes and greens.*

Diet was better, but country remedies were still magical. Living toads, he writes, were still laid on the skin in the hope of curing cancer.

People dosed themselves freely with various mixtures. In 1775 Parson Woodforde took '*brimstone, cream of tartar and treacle*' for 'flu. There were some operations, but no anaesthetics.

Woodforde's diary for 4th June 1776:

> *My tooth pained me all night, got up a little after five this morning and sent for one Reeves, a man who draws teeth in this parish, and at seven he came and drew my tooth, but shockingly bad indeed, he broke away a great piece of my gum and broke one of the fangs of the tooth, it gave me exquisite pain all the day after, and my face was swelled prodigiously in the evening and much pain....Gave the old man that drew it however 2s 6d [12½p]. He is too old, I think, to draw teeth, can't see very well.*

In 1791, Woodforde '*cured*' a stye on his eye by rubbing it with a black cat's tail on 11th March. It was inflamed again by 15th March, not surprisingly. On 22nd May 1799, he wrote:

> *My boy Jack had another touch of ague about noon. I gave him a dram of gin at the beginning of the fit and pushed him headlong into one of my ponds and ordered him to bed immediately and he was better after it and nothing of the cold fit after, but was very hot.*

With medical knowledge so uncertain and treatments so drastic, the concern shown by Jane Austen's characters over each other's colds becomes understandable. Colds could easily turn into pneumonia and prove fatal; a cough might be a symptom of consumption.

A university degree was considered sufficient training for the church. *'Church benefices may ... be considered as a fund for the provision of the younger sons of our gentry and nobles'*, said R. L. Edgeworth in *Essays on Professional Education*, 1812. Bishops and deans were appointed by the Crown. Vicars were appointed some by the Crown, some by Cathedral chapters, many by private patrons. Influential people with livings in their gift were expected to provide for their relatives and friends.

Provision was often meagre. Curacies could be worth as little as £30 a year. Many incumbents earned only £100, while the Archbishop of Canterbury earned £25,000. Sidney Smith (1771–1845) found a living at £500 a year, and rose to be residential canon of St Pauls at £2,000. Valuable livings might have to be purchased from the patron. Dr Grant, in *Mansfield Park*, buys the Mansfield living from Sir Thomas.

Jane Austen does not promote her country clergymen. Perhaps they stayed in their parishes like her father. Gilbert White was curate at Selborne for over forty years.

Because salaries were so low, *'pluralism'* was common. This meant holding several benefices at once and drawing income from them all. *'The gallopers'* were pluralists who hurried about on horseback to take services in their various parishes. They tried to get adjacent ones, for convenience. But even the galloper often could not manage to fulfil all his duties, and many parishes suffered neglect; church fabric and graveyards were decaying.

In 1810 the Clergy Residence Act was passed. This Act required clergy to live in their parishes, but it was not strictly observed. A Yorkshire clergyman asked William Wilberforce to help him get a dispensation for non-residence, because he disliked country life.

'Duty' does not seem to have been heavy. Woodforde did one service on Sundays, and communion only once a quarter. He bought his supplies from smugglers with undisturbed conscience. Clergymen gambled, drank, fathered illegitimate children and hunted the fox. An old song, 'The fox jumped over the parson's gate', goes:

> *The parson had a pair to wed,*
> *When the hounds came full in view.*
> *He just flung his surplice over his head,*
> *And bid 'em all adieu.*

Horace Walpole records (17th August 1777):

> *A Dr Suckling, who married a niece of my father, quarrelled with a country squire, who said, 'Doctor, your gown is your protection.'*
> *'Is that so?' replied the parson, 'but by God it shall not be yours', pulled it off and thrashed him.*

The careless behaviour of some clergy attracted criticisms. John Bowdler complained in *Reform or Ruin* (1797) that among the clergy *'luxury, corruption, adultery, gaming, pride, vanity, idleness, extravagance and dissipation prevail too generally'*.

Arthur Young's diary (29th August 1806) records that many of the clergy are *'profligate, many thoroughly worldly-minded'*. And even though some were of *'very respectable moral character'*, they were *'without a spark of vital religion'*. On 16th January that year he wrote that his neighbour Gooch, a curate (who might well, we feel, have been biased),

> *gave me 20 cases at least of rectors who ... cheat and impose on their curates, by most unworthy evasions; but if a farmer cheats them of a turnip in tithe, they pronounce them all the rogues to be imagined.*

The tithe was one-tenth of the layman's produce payable to the clergyman, a tax which in its time caused much bitterness. Tithes changed, after the enclosure of land, from produce given by the peasantry to money given by landowners. Eventually the system was abolished.

Status, income and comforts of the clergy rose during the century, but Jane Austen's clergymen seem to have been better off financially, more acceptable socially, than the average clerics of her time. Many, starting lower down on the social ladder than her younger sons, were harassed by desperate poverty. During Jane Austen's lifetime, there was a religious revival, in which she quietly shared. (See Chapter 11.) A clergyman's daughter, she took the keenest interest in the duties, and the status, of the profession.

MANSFIELD PARK

Mary Crawford regrets that Edmund is to be a clergyman. She wishes instead that he had gone into the Army at sixteen, the normal age for doing so. Commissions had to be

The Royal Naval Academy, Portsmouth, where Francis and Charles Austen received their training. Lithograph by J. T. Lee, 1806. (Portsmouth City Museums)

purchased, an innovation introduced by Charles II. He recognized, looking with hindsight at his father's fate, that any successful rising had to have the Army behind it. He argued, shrewdly, that an Army officered by young men from the wealthy classes would be less likely to revolt against the monarchy.

The Navy was officered by the sons of gentlemen who could not afford to buy them Army commissions, and offered more open prospects, as the careers of Jane Austen's own brothers, as well as the stories of *Mansfield Park* and *Persuasion*, make clear. Francis and Charles Austen went to the Royal Naval Academy at the age of twelve. Instructors were forbidden to observe distinctions of rank among the boys, and no personal servants were allowed.

Promotion was rapid in wartime. A popular naval toast was '*A bloody war and a sickly season!*'. Deaths in battle and from sickness would mean empty posts to be filled. Nelson wrote to his father:

> *I wish I could congratulate you on a rectory instead of a vicarage; it is rather awkward wishing the poor man dead, but we all rise by deaths.*

Sons of the parsonage like Nelson, both the Austen brothers became admirals. Both kept up a regular correspondence with their sisters from all over the world, and Jane Austen took a keen interest, as her letters show, in public events.

William Price in *Mansfield Park* is desperate for promotion. In peacetime, promotion was harder to get. Sir Thomas thinks it would be a good idea to introduce him to Admiral Crawford, who might be useful to him.[2] Henry Crawford secures William's promotion by influence, the usual route at the time and one which aroused resentment. Premature promotion made a few boys captains at eighteen.

Enthusiasm for the heroism of the Navy was general. Parson Woodforde's diary (29th November 1798) says:

> *Great rejoicings at Norwich today on Lord Nelson's great and noble victory over the French near Alexandria in Egypt. An ox roasted whole in the market place ... I gave my servants this evening after supper some strong beer and some punch to drink Admiral Lord Nelson's health on his late grand victory and also all the other officers with him and all the brave sailors with them and also all those brave admirals, officers and sailors that have gained such great and noble victories of late over the French.*

In 1805 the nation mourned for Nelson. Frank Austen, who missed the battle of Trafalgar because of contrary winds, wrote: *'I never heard of his equal, nor do I expect again to see such a man.'*

Francis spent four years as a midshipman. As Gisborne observed, young men were often placed in the Army and Navy *'before their education is properly completed'*. The better commanders took care of the boys under them.

Jane Austen wrote (15th October 1813) about the progress of a friend, then a midshipman.

> *When he first joined the Namur my brother did not find him forward enough to what they call put in the office, and therefore placed him under the schoolmaster, and he is very much improved, and goes into the office now every afternoon, still attending school in the morning.*

Frank Austen was noticed as *'the officer who knelt in church'* and read his Bible every day. Divine service was performed morning and evening, according to the liturgy of the Church of England, and a sermon preached on Sundays, except in bad weather. We learn from Gisborne that swearing, blasphemy and cursing the name of God were punishable, under Navy rules, by wearing a '*wooden collar*'. Punishments for officers were more lenient: commissioned officers were fined a shilling (5p), inferior officers sixpence ($2\frac{1}{2}$p). Drunken seamen were put in irons till sober; drunken officers forfeited a day's pay. '*Drunkenness and profane language*', said Gisborne, were a proverbial disgrace. The navy was '*manned by violence and maintained by cruelty*', said Admiral Vernon in 1749. The violence was that of the Press Gang.

Fanny, Mr Price and Henry Crawford take walks on the ramparts in Portsmouth. From E. D. Clarke's *A Tour of the South of England* (1793) we learn they were worth seeing.

Portsmouth is, he says,

> *the key of England. Its noble haven, capable of containing a thousand sail of the line; its extensive fortifications, arranged and executed by engineers of the first ability; the number of its inhabitants, its dockyards, its wonderful importance to Great Britain, render it the admiration of Europe...a first-rate man of war may always float in safety....The mouth of the harbour is fortified by a ... castle ... fortified with a double moat, pallisadoes, ravelins, and a counterscarp, from which there are several advanced works, to cover the fort against the approach of an enemy ... on the opposite side ... there is another platform, of twenty great guns....*

England needed these defences. Sir Thomas runs into a '*French privateer*' on his way home from the West Indies.[3]

PERSUASION

The novel is set in 1814, a time of peace. But the fortunes have been made in the war; Captain Harville has been wounded.[4]

Captain Wentworth earns his promotion in the '*action off San Domingo*'.[5] This took place on 6th February 1806. A French squadron was caught and beaten by a fleet commanded by Sir John Duckworth. Frank Austen fought in the battle, which brought several valuable prizes. Naval fortunes were made by '*prize-money*' (from French *prise* (taken)), shared among the officers and crew.

Sir Walter Elliot objects to the Navy as

The crowded harbour at Portsmouth as seen by Thomas Rowlandson (Reproduced by courtesy of the Trustees of the British Museum)

> *the means of bringing persons of obscure birth into undue*
> *distinction, and raising men to honours which their fathers*
> *and grandfathers never dreamed of ... Lord St Ives, whose*
> *father we all know to have been a country curate, without*
> *bread to eat....*[6]

When we remember that Jane Austen's own brave and successful sailor brothers were, like Nelson, the sons of a country clergyman, we are in no doubt as to what attitude the author takes to Sir Walter's grotesque snobbery.

A Mrs Barrett, who knew Jane Austen, said: '*Anne Elliot was herself; her enthusiasm for the navy, and her perfect unselfishness, reflect her completely.*'

Anne Elliot is a reader of newspapers, well-informed on all Naval matters. She defends the Navy against her father: '*Sailors work hard enough for their comforts, we must all allow.*'[7]

Lady Russell objected to Frederick Wentworth because he was not well-connected and his prospects were uncertain. But he '*was brilliant, he was headstrong*'[8] and eventually '*distinguished himself*'.[9] Eventually he and Anne are reunited. Jane Austen is on the side of the energetic self-made hero, against the static exclusiveness of Sir Walter and Lady Russell.

> Anne *gloried in being a sailor's wife, but she must pay the tax of quick alarm for belonging to that profession which is, if possible, more distinguished in its domestic virtues than in its national importance.*[10]

These are the closing words of Jane Austen's last novel.

Reading Jane Austen carefully with some knowledge of the background she assumed her readers would share, it is impossible to accept the common objections that she was a snob, and that she ignored the public events of her day. The Napoleonic Wars, the economic and social changes she lived through, are there in the books, part of the lives of her characters. In depicting women as leading lives restricted in scope, she reflected reality. But she and Anne Elliot looked out on to the wider world and took intelligent account of it.

[1] Jane Austen *Emma* p. 92 [2] Jane Austen *Mansfield Park* p. 266 [3] *ibid*. p. 18 [4] Jane Austen *Persuasion* p. 94 [5] *ibid*. p. 26 [6] *ibid*. p. 19 [7] *ibid*. p. 19 [8] *ibid*. p. 27 [9] *ibid*. p. 29 [10] *ibid*. p. 252

8

London and Bath

Towns were growing fast as country folk moved to look for work. The process had been going on all through the eighteenth century. In *Humphry Clinker* (1771) Matthew Bramble says many of these people became *'thieves and sharpers; and London being an immense wilderness, in which there is neither watch nor ward of any signification, nor any order or police, affords them lurking-place as well as prey'*. There were no police till 1829. London stretched from Wapping in the east to Knightsbridge barracks in the west, and ended at Bloomsbury in the north. The country parish of Clapham still paid a shilling bounty for every polecat killed and fourpence each for hedgehogs. But Matthew Bramble predicts, accurately, that soon *'the whole county of Middlesex will be covered with brick'*.

In 1783 a commentator observed that almost every house now had a gas lamp with two wicks, with sewers and piped water *'three times a week for the trifling expense of three shillings per quarter'*. But all was not progress and comfort. The Rev. William Gilpin, a writer Jane Austen admired, wrote:

> *London comes on apace, and all those disgusting ideas, with which its great avenues abound—brick-kilns steaming with offensive smoke—sewers and ditches sweating with filth— heaps of collected soil, and stinks of every denomination, clouds of dust, rising and vanishing from agitated wheels, pursuing each other in rapid motion.*

'Collected soil' means 'night-soil' or human excrement, which was piled into heaps in the street, the 'dust-heaps' Charles Dickens was to write about in *Our Mutual Friend* (1864).

It was not surprising that those who could afford it preferred their country estates. Jane Austen seems to have preferred the dignity and tranquillity of country life to the restless bustle of towns. Sophisticated characters like the Crawfords, in *Mansfield Park*, who bring their town ways into the countryside, are deceitful and mercenary, and ultimately disruptive. During the course of the novel, Mr Crawford visits Bath and comes back talking about it, but we do not see him there. In *Northanger Abbey* and *Persuasion*, however, much of the action is set in Bath itself. It was an important provincial centre of fashion, attractive because living was cheaper than in London.

Bath as we know it was built between 1705 and 1810. Formerly a small, dirty town infested with footpads, it rose in importance as an inland resort when two temples and a magnificent Roman bath were discovered near the Abbey churchyard. The architect John Wood, who died in 1765, designed Queen Square, the Royal Crescent, the North and South parades and the exquisite Circus, built by his son of the same name. Horace Walpole wrote to Miss Mary Berry on 8th June 1791: '*Bath shoots out into new crescents, circuses and squares every year.*'

People went to Bath for health as well as fashion. J. Macky, in *A Journey through England* (1782) wrote:

> The Bath lies very low; is but a small city, but very compact; and one can hardly imagine it could accommodate near the company that frequent it, at least three parts of the year. I have been told of 8,000 families there at a time, some for the benefit of drinking its hot waters, others for bathing, and others for diversion and pleasure.

Eighteenth-century people took to '*the waters*' with enthusiasm. John Byng wrote:

> I cannot help deploring the desertion of the country by the gentlemen ... these were the supporters of the poor, and of their rights; and their wives were the Lady Bountifuls of the parish.... But since ... turnpike roads, and that all gentlemen have the gout, and all ladies the bile, it has been found necessary to fly to the bath and to sea-bathing for relief.

During the eighteenth and nineteenth centuries many spa towns grew rich from visitors in search of health. Today's equivalent is possibly the 'health farm' where people go to starve and lose weight. '*The waters*' were considered good for gout, a common eighteenth-century complaint. Symptoms are painful swelling of the joints, restlessness, irritability, cramp, indigestion, constipation and thirst. It is commonly believed to be associated with heavy drinking, especially of port, but though its

The Comforts of Bath The 1798 aquatint by Thomas Rowlandson shows a gouty old man sitting to have his portrait drawn, while his wife meets a lover behind the door. (The Fotomas Index)

eighteenth-century prevalence may have been due to the drunken habits of the time, it has recently been suggested that, like the gravel and kidney stones, gout is in part caused by dietary deficiencies. Teetotallers can and do get gout.

Jane Austen did not care for Bath. When her father retired in 1801, the family left Steventon, Jane's childhood home. Mrs Austen told her daughters: *'Well, girls! It is all settled. We have decided to leave Steventon and go to Bath.'* Jane fainted.

Having arrived there, she wrote to Cassandra (5th May 1801):

> *The first view of Bath in fine weather does not answer my expectations; I think I see more distinctly through rain ... the appearance ... was all vapour, shadow, smoke and confusion.*

Bath had its compensations, though:

> *I am not without hopes of tempting Mrs Lloyd to settle in Bath; meat is only 8d per pound, butter 12d, and cheese 9½d. You must carefully conceal from her, however, the exorbitant price of fish: a salmon has been sold at 2s 9d the whole fish. ...*

Two views of Bath are entertainingly juxtaposed in Tobias Smollett's novel, *Humphry Clinker*, written four years before Jane Austen was born. Smollett's middle-aged, irascible Matthew Bramble sees only noise, overcrowding and dangers to health, but to his niece, Lydia, Bath is '*an earthly paradise*', with waters '*hot and sparkling from the pump*'.

Her uncle is cynically afraid that this water swallowed by the patients in the pump room is '*the scourings of the bathers*', among whom he sees a child '*full of scrophulous ulcers*'. (Smollett was a medical man by profession.)

> *The water contains nothing but a little salt, and calcarious earth ... the dirt, the stench, the chilling blasts, and perpetual rains ... render this place ... intolerable.*

He complains of mud and slime below the windows of the pump room.

J. Macky writes:

> *The smoke and slime of the waters, the promiscuous multitude of people in the Bath, with nothing but their heads and hands above water, with the height of the walls that environ the bath, gave me a lively idea of several pictures I had seen of Angelo's in Italy, of Purgatory, with heads and hands uplifted in the midst of the smoke.*

The Pump Room and colonnade, Bath. Drawing by Spornberg, 1801

At the ball Matthew attends, the smell makes him feel sick:

> ...*putrid gums, imposthumated lungs, sour flatulencies, rank arm-pits, sweating feet ... such is the fragrant air we breathe in the polite assemblies of Bath.*

Other diversions were concerts, lectures on the arts and sciences, visiting the bookshops and plays.

Matthew objects that

> *a very inconsiderable proportion of genteel people are lost in a mob of impudent plebeians, who have neither understanding nor judgement, nor the least idea of propriety and decorum ... a mushroom of opulence, who pays his cook seventy guineas a week for ... one meal a day.* There were '*negro-drivers*' and '*hucksters*', '*men of low birth and no breeding ... suddenly translated into a state of affluence*' by the '*general tide of luxury*'.

NORTHANGER ABBEY

Bath was still socially mixed in the 1790s, when *Northanger Abbey* was written; Mr Allen, the squire of the village, goes to Bath for his gout, and generously takes the parson's daughter, Catherine, with him and his wife. In the public rooms she meets the Thorpes, children of a lawyer, and Henry Tilney, the son of a great landowner. Henry is introduced to her by the master of ceremonies.

On the evidence of *Northanger Abbey*, it was the custom to dance two dances and then change partners, but the rule was not rigidly adhered to. Catherine can, within the bounds of politeness, refuse to dance again with John Thorpe, since '*our two dances are over*'; on the other hand, Isabella boasts that Catherine's brother James '*wants me to dance with him again, although I tell him that it is a most improper thing, and entirely against the rules ...*'. James retorts: '*... in these public assemblies it is as often done as not.*'[1]

Gisborne writes of the '*present custom of changing partners at stated intervals*' but does not specify. He writes of dancing in a way which recalls Mr Collins in *Pride and Prejudice*:

> *...an amusement ... both innocent and salubrious, and therefore by no means improper, under suitable regulations, to constitute the occasional entertainment of youth.*

The Assembly Rooms at Bath, where Catherine Morland met Henry Tilney. From J. C. Nattes's *Bath*, 1806.

Axford and Paragon Buildings, Bath. Jane Austen stayed at Paragon in 1801. From J. C. Nattes's *Bath*, 1806.

The new dance was the waltz, towards the end of the War. This was not the so-called 'modern waltz' of the first half of the twentieth century, in which the woman was steered backwards, but a rapid whirling movement, the so-called 'old-time waltz'. The minuet was still danced, but was considered old-fashioned.

PERSUASION

Anne Elliot plays the piano for others to dance to, symbolic of her spinster role in life. She moves to Bath when her father, Sir Walter, can no longer afford to keep up his estate. Anne, like Jane Austen, dislikes Bath.

The great weakness of Elizabeth and her father is their concern for outward appearances. Sir Walter wishes Lady Russell would wear rouge, and recommends the use of '*Gowland*' to Mrs Clay for her freckles. This was a puzzle till the late, tireless Dr R. W. Chapman discovered a contemporary advertisement:

> *Mrs Vincent Gowland's lotion ... the most pleasant and effectual remedy for all complaints to which the face and skin are liable ... in quarts 8s. 6d.* [42½p]

This tendency is exaggerated when they move to Bath. The city brings out the worst in Elizabeth Elliot, Anne's elder sister, and makes her betray the social obligations of her class, the duties of hospitality.

> *Elizabeth felt that Mrs Musgrave and all her party ought to be asked to dine with them, but she could not bear to have the difference of style, the reduction of servants, which a dinner must betray, witnessed by those who had been always so inferior to the Elliots of Kellynch. It was a struggle between propriety and vanity; but vanity got the better ...Old fashioned notions—country hospitality—we do not profess to give dinners—few people in Bath do—Lady Alicia never does; did not even ask her own sister's family, though they were here a month.*[2]

In post-war Bath, the refined classes did not go to the public rooms. '*The theatre or the rooms*' where Captain Wentworth, the man Anne loves, '*was most likely to be, were not fashionable enough for the Elliots, whose evening amusements were solely in the elegant stupidity of private parties*'.[3]

Anne does not care, either, for Bath's evening parties: '*I am no card player.*'[4]

Jane Austen's letters often express similar boredom. On 12th May 1801, she writes to Cassandra from Bath:

> *Another stupid party last night. Perhaps if they were larger they might be less intolerable, but here there were only just enough to make one card table, with six people to look on, and talk nonsense to each other.*

In the same letter she wrote:

> *I am proud to say that I have a very good eye at an Adultress, for though repeatedly assured that another in the same party was the* She, *I fixed on the right one from the first. . . . She is not so pretty as I expected ; her face has the same defect of baldness as her sister's, and her features not so handsome ; she was highly rouged, and looked rather quietly and contentedly silly than anything else. Mrs Badcock and two young women were of the same party, except when Mrs Badcock thought herself obliged to leave them to run round the room after her drunken husband.*

Drunkenness was common. Samuel Rogers tells a story about Dr Fordyce (not the clergyman, but a medical man, author of a treatise on the medicinal uses of rhubarb), who

> *sometimes drank a good deal at dinner. He was summoned one evening to see a lady patient when he was more than half-seas-over, and conscious that he was so. Feeling her pulse, and finding himself unable to count its beats, he muttered, 'Drunk, by God !' Next morning, recollecting the circumstance, he was greatly vexed ; and just as he was thinking what explanation of his behaviour he should offer to the lady, a letter from her was put into his hand. 'She too well knew,' said the letter, 'that he had discovered the unfortunate condition in which she was when he last visited her ; and she entreated him to keep the matter secret in consideration of the enclosed (a hundred pound banknote).'*

[1] Jane Austen *Northanger Abbey* p. 57   [2] Jane Austen *Persuasion* p. 219   [3] *ibid.* p. 180   [4] *ibid.* p. 225

9

Improvements

Edmund Burke wrote:

> *It is with infinite caution that any man ought to venture upon pulling down an edifice, which has answered in any tolerable degree for ages the common purposes of society, or of building it up again, without having models and patterns of approved utility before his eyes.*

Yet, during the eighteenth century in which he lived, people demolished and modernized recklessly, moved tons of earth to create smooth hills, looking down on distant artificial lakes, with false bridges at the end of them, the whole surrounded not by fences, but ha-has or invisible ditches. Old-fashioned Elizabethan or 'Dutch' gardens in geometric patterns, like the ones at Hampton Court, were despised, and rooted up by professional 'improvers'.

Isaac Ware, in *A Complete Body of Architecture* (1756) explained that the idea was '*to collect the beauties of nature ... without that formality which was once understood to constitute the character of a garden ...*'.

Writing of one of the earliest landscape gardeners, Horace Walpole said:

> *The great principles on which he worked were perspective, and light and shade. Groups of trees broke too uniform or too extensive a lawn ... where the view was ... too much exposed ... he blotted out some parts by thick shades, to divide it into variety, or to make the richest scene more enchanting ... he realised the compositions of the greatest masters of painting.*

Gilpin wrote that the smoothness of a garden made no figure on canvas. But

> *turn the lawn into a piece of broken ground; plant rugged oaks instead of flowering shrubs; break the edges of the*

> *walk; ...mark it with wheel tracks ... instead of making*
> *the whole smooth, make it rough, and you also make it*
> *picturesque.*

Some people went rather far in their pursuit of the picturesque. Lady Dunmore, daughter of the Duke of Hamilton, told Samuel Rogers that her father advertised for *'a hermit'* as a walking ornament for his pleasure grounds. The advertisement laid down that the hermit should shave once a year, and then not completely. Whether the Duke found his hermit we do not know.

A friend, calling on him one day, asked if it was true that he kept a tame tiger—*'He immediately slapped his thigh and uttered a sort of whistle; and forth crept the long-backed animal from under the sofa.'*

Jane West gives us a glimpse of what gardens must have looked like:

> *If you fetch your models from countries ignorant of just*
> *proportion and correct design, mandarins, dragons and*
> *pagodas may be purchased; pyramids and sphinxes may be*
> *procured.*

The eighteenth century saw people starting to build on hilltops, for a view. Writing to George Montague on 25th July 1748, Walpole describes Gossfield, Nugent's seat, being modernized.

> *The park ... is to be sixteen hundred acres, and is bounded*
> *with a wood of five miles round; and the lake, which is very*
> *beautiful, is of seventy acres, directly in a line with the*
> *house, at the bottom of a fine lawn, and broke with very*
> *pretty groves.... The house is vast ... all modernised but in*
> *patches, and in the bad taste that came between the*
> *charming venerable gothic and pure architecture.*

Gossfield must have been Tudor or Jacobean; by *'pure architecture'* Walpole means the neo-classical style of the Italian architect Palladio (1518–80) in Vicenza.

On 15th June 1768, Walpole writes:

> *They cry 'This is a bad summer' as if we ever had any other*
> *... we ruin ourselves with inviting over foreign trees, and*
> *make our houses clamber up hills to look at*
> *prospects.... How our ancestors would laugh at us, who*
> *knew there was no being comfortable, unless you had a high*
> *hill before your nose, and a thick warm wood at your back.*

Taste, he predicts, will not last: it is too chilly and uncomfortable.

Old-fashioned estates had been admired for their avenues and thick woodlands. Now fashion and economic advantage combined to fell them. Nelson was short of timber to build ships to fight the French, and fashionable theories of the picturesque preferred 'clumps' of trees scattered over smooth grassland. Ancient woodlands were sacrificed wholesale for quick profits.

MANSFIELD PARK

Mr Rushworth, the foolish owner of Sotherton, thinks his estate could do with modernization. He has a friend whose house and grounds have been done by Humphrey Repton and decides to call Repton in himself. Mr Rushworth says that his friend has had

> two or three fine old trees cut down that grew too near the house, and it opens the prospect amazingly, which makes me think that Repton, or any body of that sort, would certainly have the avenue at Sotherton down. . . .

Fanny says:

> 'Cut down an avenue! What a pity! Does it not make you think of Cowper? "Ye fallen avenues once more I mourn your fate unmerited." '[1]

The Rev. William Gilpin had quoted these lines in his *Observations on the Western Parts of England, Relative Chiefly to Picturesque Beauty*.

Humphrey Repton really existed. We learn from *Mansfield Park* that his terms were five guineas (£5.25p) a day, then an enormous sum.[2] Repton's cry was *'break the avenue'*. He started out by attacking all symmetry, but ended up laying out *'knot gardens'*, with patterns copied from the backgrounds of old portraits, when fashion returned to what it had formerly despised.

Repton is satirized in Thomas Love Peacock's novel, *Headlong Hall* (1816), as 'Mr Milestone'.

> 'My dear sir,' said Mr Milestone, 'accord me your permission to wave the wand of enchantment over your grounds. The rocks shall be blown up, the trees shall be cut

> *down, the wilderness and all its goats shall vanish like mist.*
> *Pagodas and Chinese bridges, gravel walks and shrubberies,*
> *bowling-greens, canals and clumps of larch, shall rise upon*
> *its ruins. One age, sir, has brought to light the treasures of*
> *ancient learning; a second has penetrated into the depths of*
> *metaphysics; a third has brought to perfection the science of*
> *astronomy; but it was reserved for the exclusive genius of*
> *the present times, to invent the noble art of picturesque*
> *gardening, which has given, as it were, a new tint to the*
> *complexion of nature, and a new outline to the physiognomy*
> *of the universe.'*

Mr Milestone's opponent, Sir Patrick O'Prism, is based on Sir
Uvedale Price, Bart., who wrote an essay on 'the picturesque' in
which he argued for natural, as against formally arranged,
beauty. Sir Patrick O'Prism quotes Gilpin:

> *...your system of levelling and trimming and clipping, and*
> *docking, and clumping, and polishing, and cropping, and*
> *shaving, destroys all beautiful intricacies of natural*
> *luxuriance, and all the graduated harmonies of light and*
> *shade, melting into one another, as you see them on that*
> *rock over yonder.*

Sir Patrick compares improved places to *'sheets of green paper*
...like Hounslow Heath, thinly sprinkled over with bushes and high-
waymen'. (Both Gilpin and Horace Walpole disapproved of the
excessive tidying-up carried out by Capability Brown and his
successors.)

Mr Milestone challenges Sir Patrick to distinguish between
the picturesque and the beautiful. Sir Patrick agrees with Sir
Joshua Reynolds that the distinction is without a difference. Sir
Patrick says the beautiful is *'that which pleases the eye. And what*
pleases the eye? Tints variously broken and blended. Now tints
variously broken and blended constitute the picturesque.'

Mary Crawford calls her brother Henry a *'capital improver'*,
but his ideas for improvement at Thornton Lacy, which will be
Edmund's parsonage house, are ironically treated by Jane
Austen.

Henry's ideas mean five years' work; the farmyard is *'a terrible*
nuisance'. He wants to clear it away, plant trees to hide the
blacksmith's shop. (A blacksmith's shop then was no picturesque
survival, but an everyday utility, like a filling station today.)

Henry wants to '*turn the house round*' and put a new garden at the back, buy adjoining land and alter the course of the stream. Henry is concerned only with appearances.

Edmund's reply to such extravagant folly is that he must be '*satisfied with rather less ornament and beauty*'.[3]

Sotherton is '*amply furnished in the taste of fifty years back, with shining floors, solid mahogany, rich damask, marble, gilding and carving*'.[4] Maria is '*glad the church is not so close to the great house as often happens in old places*'.[5] This is a pointer against Maria. At Mansfield, which is to be spiritually revived by the installation of Edmund and Fanny in the parsonage house, the church and house are physically not far apart, and by Edmund's ordination are symbolically brought together.

Whereas Mary Crawford saw '*nature, inanimate nature, with little observation*', Fanny observes '*the appearance of the country, the bearings of the roads, the difference of soil, the state of harvest, the cottages, the cattle, the children*'.[6] She looks for the combination of beauty with utility. Edmund agrees with Fanny that those who have not at least been given a taste for nature in early life lose a great deal. Jane Austen herself said she looked forward to beauty of landscape as one of the joys of heaven. Like Gilpin before her, however, she seems to have preferred it untouched by the hand of the improver.

Lyme Regis, Dorset, as Jane Austen would have seen it. Etching and aquatint by R. Cruikshank, 1819 (The Fotomas Index)

PERSUASION

Jane Austen's views on 'improvements' are made equally clear in *Persuasion*, where she gives us a piece of descriptive landscape writing about Lyme Regis.

> ...*the Cobb itself, with its old wonders and new improvements, with the very beautiful line of cliffs stretching out to east of the town, are what the stranger's eye will seek; and a very strange stranger it must be, who does not see charms in the immediate environs of Lyme, to make him wish to know it better. The scenes in its neighbourhood, Charmouth, with its high grounds and excessive sweeps of country, and still more its sweet, retired bay, backed by dark cliffs, where fragments of low rock among the sands make it the happiest spot for watching the flow of the tide, for sitting in unwearied contemplation; —the woody varieties of the cheerful village of Up Lyme, and, above all, Pinny, with its green chasms between romantic rocks, where the scattered forest trees and orchards of luxuriant growth declare that many a generation must have passed away since the first partial falling of the cliff prepared the ground for such a state, where a scene so wonderful and so lovely is exhibited ... these places must be visited, and visited again, to make the worth of Lyme understood.*[7]

'New improvements' are for passing strangers. It is the reflective visitor alone, who has visited and visited again, who can understand the worth of Lyme. Jane Austen can appreciate, with her own generation, the '*green chasms*' and '*romantic rocks*', and draw from them, by '*unwearied contemplation*', the conclusion that while the town offers bustle and modernity, and the generations pass away, the beauty of nature outlasts them.

In the same book, we get an ironical view of 'improvement' brought about by increasing prosperity, and the progressive refinement of a family who sweep away the old ways and old furniture in accordance with fashion.

> *To the Great House accordingly they went, to sit the full half hour in the old-fashioned square parlour, with a small carpet and shining floor, to which the present daughters of the house were gradually giving the proper air of confusion by a grand piano forte and a harp, flower-stands and little*

A nobleman improving his estate by Thomas Rowlandson. The title is richly ironic. The nobleman, accompanied by his lady and their chaplain (with dogs), inspects plans, while real or fake lumps of classical pillar are hauled about, and a mason works to create an urn in the classical style (left). It is all very expensive.

*tables placed in every direction. Oh! could the originals of
the portraits against the wainscot, could the gentlemen in
brown velvet and the ladies in blue satin have seen what was
going on, have been conscious of such an overthrow of all
order and neatness.*

*The Musgroves, like their houses, were in a state of
alteration,* perhaps of improvement. *The father and
mother were in the old English style, and the young people
in the new. Mr and Mrs Musgrove were a very good sort of
people ; friendly and hospitable, not much educated, and not
at all elegant. Their children had more modern minds and
manners ... Henrietta and Louisa, young ladies of nineteen
and twenty ... had brought from a school at Exeter all the
usual stock of accomplishments* but Anne *would not have
given up her own more elegant and cultivated mind for all
their enjoyments.*[8]

Humphrey Repton wrote, in his *Fragments on the Theory of
Modern Gardening* (1816),

*No more the cedar parlour's formal gloom
With dulness chills, 'tis now the living room
Where guests to whim, to taste or fancy true
Scattered in groups, their different plans pursue.*

Jane Austen preferred the tried and true to innovations.

Anne is cultivated in that she can enjoy with the beauty of
autumn the *'poetical sweets'* her reading has given her. Like her
author, she contemplates the rhythm of the seasons and
meditates on time and change. Anne has true taste, free of
superlatives and rapture. She truly recognizes the responsibilities
of her rank. Her father and sisters think only of their status.

Jane Austen liked her gentry to be resident, living comfortably
in their old houses, surrounded by fine timbers which neither
economy nor fashion has rooted up, taking care of their tenants
and preserving their heritage for future generations.

Edmund Burke wrote:

*A spirit of innovation is generally the result of a selfish
temper and confined views. People will not look forward to
posterity, who never look backward to their ancestors.*

[1] Jane Austen *Mansfield Park* p. 56 [2] *ibid.* p. 53 [3] *ibid.* p.
242 [4] *ibid.* p. 84 [5] *ibid.* p. 82 [6] *ibid.* p. 81 [7] Jane Austen
Persuasion pp. 95–6 [8] *ibid.* p. 40

10

A passion for dead leaves

In *Northanger Abbey*, the Tilneys, young people of discernment and taste, go for a walk in the environs of Bath. Their conversation and appreciation of the countryside open Catherine's eyes, and teach her to look differently at landscape.

> *It seemed as if a good view were no longer to be taken from the top of an high hill, and that a clear blue sky was no longer a proof of a fine day.*[1]

Low points for looking at views were preferred to panoramic vistas. The fondness for clouds goes back to Burke's *Enquiry Into the Sublime and the Beautiful* (1757):

> *An immense mountain covered with a shining green turf is nothing ... to one dark and gloomy; the cloudy sky is more grand than the blue.*

The Tilneys look at nature in the way taught by art masters, because they are skilled in the accomplishment of drawing. Henry

> *talked of foregrounds, distances, and second distances; sidescreens and perspectives; lights and shades; and Catherine was so hopeful a scholar, that when they gained the top of Beechen Cliff, she voluntarily rejected the whole city of Bath as unworthy to make part of a landscape.*[2]

The joke is at Catherine's expense. The city of Bath, viewed from above, is still beautiful today. It was much more so at the beginning of the nineteenth century, when its neo-classical centre was surrounded by wooded hills, instead of sprawling suburbs.

Henry continues to point out to Catherine the beauties of nature, but falls into the serious issues of the day, as befits a man of intellect and wide interests:

> *... by an easy transition from a piece of rocky fragment and the withered oak which he had placed near its summit, to*

> *oaks in general, to forests, the inclosure of them, waste*
> *lands, crown lands and government ....*[3]

Catherine looks forward to exploring Blaize Castle, which she imagines will be like the castle of Udolpho. (See Chapter 6) '*She cared for no furniture of a more modern date than the fifteenth century.*'[4]

She is disappointed, too, in Northanger Abbey itself; she hopes for '*painted*' (stained) '*glass, dirt and cobwebs*'. The Gothic arches have been preserved, but the panes are clear. Fascination with old churches and tombs was typical of the age. It derived partly from Horace Walpole, whose taste was as influential in his age as that of Sir John Betjeman in ours. Walpole was against restoration and modernization.

John Byng agrees. Writing from Lewes, Sussex, in 1788, he says:

> *The ancient church of St John has lately undergone a*
> *destructive reparation (destructive I mean to the antiquary)*
> *for then all the brasses, stained glass, and anything*
> *moveable, fall a prey to the masons and glaziers.*

Walpole's interest in churches was antiquarian rather than devotional. Writing to Richard Bentley in September 1753, Walpole says of Worcester:

> *The cathedral is pretty, and has several tombs, and clusters*
> *of light pillars of Derbyshire marble, lately cleaned.*
> *Gothicism and the restoration of that architecture, and not*
> *of the bastard breed, spreads extremely in this part of the*
> *world.*

He liked the '*painted glass*' in nearby Malvern Abbey, but complained:

> *The portraits are so high, I could not distinguish them.*
> *Besides, the woman who showed me the church would pester*
> *me with Christ and King David, when I was hunting for*
> *John of Gaunt and King Edward.*

Walpole built himself a delicious Gothic house of '*the bastard breed*', called Strawberry Hill, at Twickenham, now St Mary's College of Education. Travelling in France on his Grand Tour, in 1739, Walpole describes Versailles as

Bath from above, 1817. Coloured aquatint (Reproduced by courtesy of the Trustees of the British Museum)

> ...a garden for a great child. Such was Louis Quatorze, who is here seen in his proper colours ... left to the pursuit of his own puerile ideas of glory.

This is an amazing judgment from the architect of Strawberry Hill, with its octagonal library, Gothic arched windows, and sham battlements.

He liked, though, the Convent of Chartreuse:

> All the inconveniences ... are assembled here, that melancholy meditation, selfish devotion, and despair would require. But yet 'tis pleasing. Soften the terms, and mellow the uncouth horror ... but a little, and 'tis a charming solitude. It ... is old and irregular. The chapel is gloomy: behind it, through some dark passages, you pass into a large obscure hall, which looks like a combination chamber for some hellish council.

These are the sort of notions, become the commonplaces of the next two generations, that Catherine is measuring her experiences by. Jane Austen, her brother Henry tells us, was 'at an early age ... enamoured of Gilpin on the picturesque'. The Rev. William Gilpin (1724–1804) seems to have popularized the influential term, 'picturesque', meaning 'that which would look good *in a picture'*. Gilpin was an amateur artist of considerable skill. He was born in Cumberland, which formed his taste for impressive landscapes. He and his contemporaries looked at nature and measured it against the standards of the best landscape paintings. But nature was God's work of art and therefore superior to any work of man: natural scenery was a suitable object of reverence, lifting the contemplative mind through rapture up to God.

Sir Joshua Reynolds (1723–92) said beauty and the picturesque were the same thing. Gilpin disagreed. *'Smoothness'* belonged to beauty; *'roughness'* was picturesque and suited to painting. The picturesque meant nature that looked like existing pictures. Gilpin admired strong delineation, roughness, ruggedness, variety, irregularity, crookedness. In *Instructions for Examining Landscape* Gilpin says that in inferior kinds of landscape, it is permissible to admire such *'low vulgarisms'* as *'cottages—haymaking—harvesting—and other employments of husbandry.'*

SENSE AND SENSIBILITY

Marianne's notions are all taken from Gilpin. Jane Austen holds them up to criticism, through Edward Ferrars, showing her recognition that the merely aesthetic approach is inadequate. Jane Austen knew that haymaking and harvesting were not pictures on a screen for dilettanti to enthuse over, but the backbreaking livelihoods of the rural poor.

Edward Ferrars enjoys an extensive view from a hilltop, although unselective vistas were no longer fashionable. Marianne starts to question him, and he says:

> *'You must not inquire too far, Marianne—remember I have no knowledge of the picturesque, and I shall offend you with my ignorance and want of taste.... I shall call hills steep, which ought to be bold; surfaces strange and uncouth, which ought to be irregular and rugged; and distant objects out of sight, which ought only to be indistinct through the soft medium of a hazy atmosphere.'*

For someone who claims no knowledge of the picturesque, Edward shows a surprisingly easy command of its vocabulary. Jane Austen suggests the terms are not really so difficult. Edward continues:

> '*You must be satisfied with such admiration as I can honestly give. I call it a very fine country—the hills are steep, the woods seem full of fine timber, and the valley looks comfortable and snug—with rich meadows and several neat farmhouses.... It exactly answers my idea of a fine country, because it unites beauty with utility—and I daresay it is ... picturesque ... too, because you admire it: I can easily believe it to be full of rocks and promontories, grey moss and brush wood, but these are all lost on me.*'

Edward looks at the country from the traditional standpoint, not of a man of feeling, but of the landowning country gentleman. He considers its possibilities for the rural economy, its provision for employments and its profits for landlords. '*Fine timber*' was a leading economic asset. '*Neat farmhouses*' are desirable, indicating prosperity and responsible stewardship of landholdings, in contrast to the decay pictured in *The Deserted Village.* '*Neatness*' is incompatible with poverty.

Marianne admits that '*the admiration of landscape scenery is become a mere jargon*'.

Edward explains:

> '*I like a fine prospect, but not on picturesque principles. I do not like crooked, twisted, blasted trees. I admire them much more if they are tall, straight and flourishing* [that is, saleable]. *I do not like ruined, tattered cottages. I am not fond of nettles, or thistles, or heath blossoms. I have more pleasure in a snug farmhouse than a watchtower—and a troop of tidy, happy villagers please me better than the finest banditti in the world.*'[5]

Gilpin thought figures improved a landscape. They '*break harsh lines—point out paths over mountains or to castles...give an idea of scale...add...animation*'. But some figures were out.

> *No ladies with their parasols—no white-robed misses ambling two by two—no children drawn about in their little coaches, have admittance here.*

Real people earning their livings would '*vulgarise*'. '*Milkmaids ... ploughmen, reapers, and ... peasants ... we disallow....In wild, and desert scenes, we are best pleased with banditti-soldiers.*' Surely we agree with Edward that prosperous villagers are preferable to Gilpin's frivolous and irresponsible beauty-loving.

Marianne is amazed, sorry for her sister, who laughs. Clearly we are to smile with Elinor and agree that while raggedness may be picturesque, social conscience prefers tidiness. Elinor gently teases Marianne: '*It is not everyone who has your passion for dead leaves.*'[6]

Edward has assured Marianne that if she should inherit a fortune, '*she would have every book that tells us how to admire an old twisted tree*'.[7] Rocky fragments and withered oaks were standard objects for admiration, together with everything dark, wild, lonely and mouldering. These tastes had become a cult. Gilpin discusses the picturesque qualities of the '*blasted tree*' in *Remarks on Forest Scenery (Relative Chiefly to Picturesque Beauty)*, 1791. The paintings of Salvator Rosa, with their twisted trees, ruined cottages, rocks and cliffs, were much admired.

Gilpin was cool, only partially approving:

> *I can give no reason why a cottage may not make a pleasing picture ... my eye is so captivated with sublime subjects, that it will bear no other ... the cottage offends. It should be a castle, a bridge, an aqueduct, or some other object which suits its dignity.*

Even better were ruins, best of all a ruined castle.

The impersonal narrative voice is used to describe Barton Cottage, but the implied disappointment must be Marianne's:

> *As a house, Barton Cottage, though small, was comfortable and compact; but as a cottage it was defective, for the building was regular, the roof tiled, the window shutters were not painted green, nor were the walls covered with honeysuckle.*[8]

Jane Austen admired Gilpin, but her sympathies embrace both the youthful enthusiasm of Marianne and the corrective common sense of Edward, who sees through the jargon of 'taste'. The author tells us his '*understanding was good, and his education had given it solid improvement*'.[9]

Marianne, however, is afraid Edward has '*no real taste*'. For her, taste means '*rapturous delight*'. She looks for emotional excitement in nature, art, and personal relationships, agreeing in principle with the early eighteenth-century critic John Dennis that '*poetry unless it is transporting is abominable*'. Elinor, though, says Edward has '*an innate propriety and simplicity of taste which in general direct him perfectly right*'.[10]

If Edward's taste was innate, he was fortunate; others had to acquire it expensively, by long study. The only way to learn about art was to go to the originals. Reproductions were limited to black and white engraved copies. Nobody in the period could be confused, as we often are, as to whether he had seen a painting, or only coloured reproductions. Our minds are stored with visual images, from posters, art books, television, cinema, photographs.

Their minds were stored with words from the poets, Shakespeare, the Bible. But this was changing. A new awareness of visual possibilities arose from the microscope and telescope and Newton's discovery that the rainbow consisted of white light refracted into its component parts. Newly self-conscious observation of nature runs through eighteenth-century poetry. There was a strong urge to particularize, to convey the uniqueness of each experience through colour and texture.

This ran counter to the classic Augustan theory, which looked for the universal, the unchanging general truth, and rejected the random, the accidental and the freakish. The painter Sir Joshua Reynolds and Dr Samuel Johnson insisted that truth was general, because God-given and eternal. Johnson laid down in *Rasselas* (1759) that the business of the poet was not to count '*the streaks of the tulip*'.

But the streaks of the tulip were what Gilpin and his successors found interesting. John Constable (1776–1837) wrote in 1821: '...*old rotten banks, slimy posts and brickwork ... made me a painter*'.

The taste for chasms, for mountainous scenery, was nourished by the Grand Tour, when young men travelled in horse-drawn carriages over the Alps to Italy. Thomas Gray wrote of the Alps in 1739: '*Not a precipice, not a torrent, not a cliff, but is pregnant with religion and poetry*'.

The same year, Horace Walpole wrote to Richard West on 28th September from a hamlet in the mountains of Savoy: '*Precipices, mountains, torrents, wolves, rumblings, Salvator Rosa — the pomp of our park and the meekness of our palace.*'

With neat wit he describes the grandeur of the scenery as his estate, and his wayside hut becomes a '*palace*' because it is rich in views. He is assimilating the magnificent wildness to the cultivated intellect. His educated eye compares the reality with the paintings of Salvator Rosa.

Two days later, he has reached Aix-in-Savoy and writes:

But the road, West, the road! winding round a prodigious mountain, and surrounded by others, all shagged with hanging woods, obscured with pines, or lost in clouds! Below, a torrent breaking through cliffs, and tumbling through fragments of rocks! Sheets of cascades forcing their silver speed down channelled precipices.... Now and then an old footbridge, with a broken rail, a leaning cross, a cottage, or the ruin of a hermitage! He adds: *This sounds too bombast and too romantic for one that has not seen it, too cold for one that has.*

Appreciation of such scenes had been influenced by seventeenth-century landscape painters, notably Jacob Van Ruysdal, many of whose pictures can be seen in London's National Gallery.

Gordale Scar, the famous beauty spot, painted by James Ward. The poet Thomas Gray, author of *Elegy in a country churchyard*, described it in 1770: 'one black and solid mass ... overshadows half the area below with its dreadful canopy.... I stayed there (not without shuddering) a full quarter of an hour, and thought my trouble richly paid for the impression will last for life.' (The Tate Gallery, London)

Writers and poets followed suit during the eighteenth century. Walpole's ecstatic way of writing was new, though by the end of the century such a response to landscape had become widespread and commonplace, the mere jargon of taste. No language would have struck enthusiasts like Marianne as *'too bombast and too romantic'*. Between 1750 and 1800 over sixty travel books of Switzerland were published in Britain.

The cold water of moderation thrown by Edward and Elinor harks back to an earlier belief in the rational, and the grave self-discipline of the moralists and sermonizers. Marianne's intensely excitable attitude to experience was linked with a new and controversial morality.

Gilpin wrote to Samuel Rogers on 29th November 1797 that *'another great criterion of excellence in works of fancy ... is the power to excite* feelings'.

How far, asks Jane Austen, should feelings be indulged? Ely Bates, in *Rural Philosophy or Reflections on Knowledge, Virtue and Happiness* (1803) wrote:

> *In the former part of the last century, it was usual with writers on moral subjects to insist much on the reason and fitness of things ... to have deserted these grounds for the sake of a theory which leaves everyone to resolve his duty by his feelings, would have been thought ... unphilosophical. How different are the times in which we live! Let them continue to feel, but feel as they ought: according to the immutable measures of truth and duty.*

Mary Wollstonecraft wrote that *'sensibility'* was the mania of the day. Women's

> *senses are inflamed, and their understandings neglected ... they become the prey of their senses, delicately termed sensibility, and are blown about by every momentary gust of feeling. Ever restless and anxious, their over-exercised sensibility ... renders them ... troublesome ... to others. All their thoughts turn on things calculated to excite emotion and feeling, when they should reason.*

This viewpoint underlies the story of Elinor and Marianne.

Jane West saw *'alarming changes'* in moral standards, which rejected the basis of religion, and really bowed *'to no other idol than selfishness'*. Lord David Cecil describes the issues between Marianne and Elinor as those between Rousseau and Dr Johnson.

Rousseau's *'natural religion'* was convenient and became smart: everything depended on the feelings and *'nature'*. Mrs West sums up the popular form of his influence: the young woman is

> *taught that the nature she inherits was originally perfect; that its present disordered state did not arise from any hereditary taint, the consequence of original rebellion but from ... ill-conceived laws, and ... restraints.... All reference to the ... grace of God and to the clear explanations which accompany Christian ethics, are systematically excluded ...the bewildered reader* confuses *'generosity, greatness of soul, liberality, benevolence'* with *'pride, pertinacity, indiscretion and extravagance'.*

Mrs West sees Rousseau's teaching as a recipe for selfishness and Jane Austen dramatizes the issue between the two sisters. The choice of subject was not original with her; various novels, now forgotten, dealt with pairs of sisters, one of whom was wildly romantic, the other sensible and discreet. *Sense and Sensibility* makes it clear that Marianne, with *'a sense of honour so keen, a generosity so romantic'*, is nevertheless selfish in indulging her feelings. Elinor's *'feelings were strong; but she knew how to control them'*.[11] Elinor suffers in silence, out of consideration for others. Marianne, repentant after her illness, admits to *'fretful selfishness'* and talks about *'making atonement to my God'*.[12]

Elinor, in her rational self-control, is wiser and more admirable than Marianne, although she seems less attractive to us. Jane Austen is not hostile to the culture of the feelings and the fancy, so long as they are under the cool, rational scrutiny of the mind and conscience. She wrote to her niece Fanny Knight on 13th March 1817:

> *You are all over imagination, so much flight of mind, such unbounded fancies, you should have such excellent judgement in what you do. Religious principle I fancy must explain it.*

[1] Jane Austen *Northanger Abbey* p. 110 [2] *ibid.* p. 111 [3] *ibid.* p. 111 [4] *ibid.* p. 182 [5] Jane Austen *Sense and Sensibility* pp. 96-7 [6] *ibid.* p. 88 [7] *ibid.* p. 92 [8] *ibid.* p. 28 [9] *ibid.* p. 15 [10] *ibid.* p. 19 [11] *ibid.* p. 6 [12] *ibid.* p. 346

11

Religion and morals

John Byng wrote on Sunday 10th June 1781, that he

> attended divine service; as irreligiously performed here, as
> at most other places. The inhabitants are of different sects;
> which is owing to the want of discipline in the church of
> England; for thither would the people flock were pluralities,
> in general, abolished, and more spiritual comfort to be had;
> which not being the case, the religious fly to other
> persuasions.

In 1788 W. Thompson wrote *(Tour of England and Scotland)*:

> Birmingham ... is very extensive, and a great part of it
> elegantly built. It contains upwards of one hundred
> thousand inhabitants, but the people are all diminutive in
> size and sickly in their appearance, from their sedentary
> employment. In Birmingham there is one very elegant and
> spacious church, three chapels and eight meeting-houses for
> Dissenters ... but the great mass of the people give
> themselves very little concern about religious matters, seldom
> if ever, going to church, and spending their Sundays ... in
> low debauchery. What religion there is in Birmingham is to
> be found among the Dissenters....About fifty years ago,
> there were only three principal or leading streets in
> Birmingham, which at this day is so crowded, and at the
> same time so extensive a town ... which illustrates ... the
> rapid increase of our manufactures and trade in steel and
> iron.

If the clergy were careless in the country, they failed
completely to organize any pastoral care for the towns. What
religion there was in towns was thus to be found among the
Dissenters, Christian sects outside the Church of England.
Religious splinter groups abounded. John Wesley noted in his
journal that in Frome, Somerset, he found '*Anabaptists, Quakers,
Presbyterians, Arians, Antinomians, Moravians and what not*'.

METHODISM

The brothers John and Charles Wesley were the sons of the Rector of Epworth in Lincolnshire. John went to Charterhouse and Christ Church, Oxford, and was ordained in 1725. For two years he helped his father, as curate.

Charles, while at Oxford, started a group who met together to study religion. Their seriousness and concern for observance earned them the nickname 'Methodists'. George Whitefield, a college servant, joined them.

The Rev. John Wesley, listening to a sermon on 24th May 1738, was 'converted'.

John Wesley, painted by Nathaniel Hone, R.A., in 1766 (National Portrait Gallery)

> *I felt my heart strangely warmed. I felt I did trust in Christ, Christ alone, for salvation; and an assurance was given me that he had taken away my sins.*

He spent the rest of his life preaching up and down the country, speaking in the open air to crowds of thousands. He convinced his audiences that 'a new birth' was possible for those who accepted the love of Christ, and that it was possible to lead a sanctified life on earth. Many, as a result, led sober and virtuous lives. *'My methodists grow diligent and frugal'*, he wrote in his diary, later in life.

John Wesley taught that Christ died for all men, and not just for the elect, arbitrarily chosen by God. Whitefield, however, followed the doctrines of John Calvin, inherited from St Augustine, that some men were predestined for salvation and others for damnation. Whitefield did not accept that it was possible to be sinless on earth.

Whitefield was supported by Selina, Countess of Huntingdon, who spread his teaching among the upper classes, and paid for buildings. A separate sect was formed, called 'Lady Huntingdon's Connexion'. She established training colleges in Wales, but when the sect bearing her name broke away from the established church, her ministers returned to the Church of England. This brought in a new strain of earnestness.

Many of the upper classes resisted Lady Huntingdon's influence. The Duchess of Buckingham wrote to her about the Methodists that their teachings were

> *repulsive and strongly tinctured with impertinence and disrespect towards their superiors, in perpetually endeavouring to level all ranks and do away with all distinctions. It is monstrous to be told you have a heart as sinful as the common wretches that crawl the earth.*

It might be Lady Catherine speaking.

EVANGELICALISM

The established clergy were suspicious of 'enthusiasm', so Methodism relied on lay preachers. But the Methodist influence gradually infiltrated and changed the Church. This was because their teaching coincided with the Evangelical doctrines, preached since Wesley was a boy, that guilt for sin, leading to repentance, could bring the sinner to God through Christ. For many eighteenth-century people a vague feeling that God was in his heaven and could be relied on to see to the eternal fitness of things had been enough. This was Deism, or natural religion.

Methodism and Evangelicalism meant a return to Christianity. They brought with them a new concern for morality, for propriety and sobriety.

Horace Walpole wrote (3rd September 1748):

> *Gumley, who you know is grown methodist, came to tell him that as he was on duty, a tree in Hyde-park near the powder magazine had been set on fire; the duke replied, he hoped it was not by* the new light. He adds: *Whitefield preaches continually at my Lady Huntingdon's in Chelsea; my Lord Chesterfield, my Lord Bath, my Lady Townshend, my Lady Thanet, and others have been to hear him.*

John Byng wrote in 1789 that Methodist clergy were considered as stumbling blocks and dangerous characters by orthodox clergy.

> *Now what the title of Methodist is meant to signify, I know not; but if these preachers do restore attention, and congregations within churches, and do preach the word of God, they appear to me as men most commendable; and as useful to the nation, by their opposition to the church ministry, in Parliament ... they are like military martinets, who are scoffed at by the ignorant, and indolent, but who preserve the army from ruin.*

In Byng's words we see the same concern for discipline and order as a bulwark against chaos which underlies Jane Austen's novels. The middle and upper classes avoided what Sidney Smith called *'the nonsense, the melancholy and the madness of the Tabernacle'*. Most remained loyal members of the Church of England, but those who were influenced by Evangelicalism were convinced that sin was real and hell eternal. One should strive and wrestle with conscience. But once certain of his faith, an Evangelical could be sure he would be saved. Unlike Whitefield's Calvinism, Methodism and Evangelicalism brought a message of hope.

Writing to Cassandra on 24th January 1809, Jane Austen wrote: *I do not like Evangelicals*. But in 1814, the year *Mansfield Park* was published, she wrote to Fanny Knight:

I am by no means convinced that we ought not all to be Evangelicals, and am at least persuaded that they who are so from Reason and Feeling must be happiest and safest.

She was thoroughly religious and devout, writes Jane Austen's brother Henry, *fearful of giving offence to God ....On serious subjects she was well-instructed, both by reading and meditation, and her opinions accorded strictly with those of our Established Church.*

MANSFIELD PARK

Jane herself said *Mansfield Park* was '*about ordination*'. Readers have doubted this, but the book shows a steady, serious concern with the duties of a parish priest. In it, she is hostile to flightiness and worldly ambition, mercenary and ambitious connections.

Dr Johnson wrote:

The Dean of Carlisle, who was then a little rector in Northamptonshire, told me, that it might be discerned whether or no there was a clergyman resident in a parish, by the civil or savage manner of the people.

Gisborne, himself a clergyman, insisted on '*the general obligation of residence*'. The resident clergyman and the resident squire could combat godlessness, lawlessness and potential revolt by setting a good example and keeping a firm hand on the reins. That Jane Austen concurred in this belief is shown by *Emma* and *Mansfield Park*.

Henry Crawford would like to rent the parsonage house at Thornton Lacey, where Edmund will be parish priest. The request is refused by Sir Thomas, as he takes it for granted, and Edmund agrees, that a priest must reside. Sir Thomas says:

A parish has wants and claims which can be known only by a clergyman constantly resident, and which no proxy can be capable of satisfying ... Edmund might, in the common phrase, do the duty of Thornton, that is, he might read prayers and preach, without giving up Mansfield Park; he might ride over, every Sunday, to a house nominally inhabited, and go through divine service; he might be the clergyman of Thornton Lacey every seventh day, for three or four hours, if that would content him. But it will not. He

*knows that human nature needs more lessons than a weekly
sermon can convey, and that if he does not live among his
parishioners and prove himself by constant attention their
well-wisher and friend, he does very little either for their
good or his own.*[1]

Henry Crawford looks on the liturgy as art and entertainment.
It *'has beauties which not even a careless, slovenly style of reading
can destroy; but it has also redundancies and repetitions...'.* Henry
is unaware of spiritual values.

His sister Mary constantly pains Edmund by mocking the
profession of clergyman and begging him to give it up. She
disqualifies herself as a wife for him with everything she says.

At Sotherton, hearing that the family chapel is hardly used
and that prayers read by the domestic chaplain have been
abandoned, Mary says: *'Every generation has its improvements.'*

Fanny regrets the change. Mary laughs, and talks about people
who *'force all the poor housemaids and footmen'* to *'say their
prayers here twice a day'*. Edmund says the master and mistress
should be there. Mary makes a long speech about the boredom
and inconvenience of religious observance, concluding *'in those
days, I fancy parsons were very inferior even to what they are now'*.[3]

Jane West noted that there were very few places where family
prayers were still preserved. Arthur Young wrote (25th April
1801) that Lord Carrington's daughter told a visitor: *'My papa
used to have prayers in his family, but none since he has been made a
peer.'*

Edmund gives Mary a lecture about being serious on serious
subjects. At that point in the story, Mary does not know that
Edmund plans to become a clergyman; but even after
discovering that he does, she continues to belittle the cloth.

Talking to Mary later, Edmund clarifies for her his ideas of
duty: a clergyman *'has the guardianship of religion and morals, and
consequently of the manners which result from their influence'*.

Mary thinks he exaggerates this influence: *'How can two
sermons a week, even suppose them worth hearing, supposing the
preacher to have the sense to prefer Blair's to his own, do all that
you speak of?'*

Blair's sermons were printed, and many clergy used such
sources. Mary assumes that it is more intelligent to use such
materials than to write one's own; this is another example of her
cynicism.

Edmund replies that the clergyman should influence public manners in the sense of

> 'conduct . . . the result of good principles; the effect, in short, of those doctrines which it is their duty to teach and recommend; and it will, I believe, be everywhere found, that as the clergy are, or are not what they ought to be, so are the rest of the nation.'[4]

Jane Austen's view of morality was traditional. Her views are clearly shown in her letters. On 20th June 1808, she wrote:

> This is a sad story about Mrs Powlett. I should not have suspected her of such a thing. She stayed the sacrament, I remember, the last time that you and I did. A hint of it, with initials, was in yesterday's Courier. . . .

A hint of Maria's elopement with Henry, with initials, appears in the London papers.

On 13th March 1817, Jane Austen wrote to Cassandra:

> If I were the Duchess of Richmond, I should be very miserable about my son's choice. What can be expected from a Paget, born and brought up in the centre of conjugal infidelity and divorces?

This sounds like a reflection of times like our own, but attitudes were different. Scandals in high life were common, as Mr Price recognizes: 'so many fine ladies were going to the devil now-a-days that way'. His response to Maria's disgrace is characteristically brutal: he'd 'give her the rope's end as long as I could stand over her'.[5]

Mary Wollstonecraft was considered by many to be a dangerous moral rebel, yet she wrote in A Vindication of the Rights of Woman:

> A Christian has still nobler motives to incite her to preserve her chastity . . . for her body has been called the temple of the living God. . . . His eye searcheth the heart . . . her chastity must be founded on modesty and not on worldly prudence.

Chastity was seen as a positive virtue, not as a matter of personal preference. We have to grasp a difference in feeling between former ages and our own to understand the standards Jane Austen was invoking.

Admiral Crawford, the uncle of Mary and Henry, was '*a man of vicious conduct, who chose ... to bring his mistress under his own roof*'.[6]

Henry Crawford admits;

> '*The admiral has his faults, but he is a very good man, and has been more than a father to me. Few fathers would have let me have my own way half so much.*'[7]

Henry's lazy tolerance, his worldly evaluation of his uncle as '*a very good man*', is an index of his moral slackness. If Henry had more principle, he would condemn his uncle's conduct, instead of being grateful for unwise indulgence. Even Lady Bertram, bone-idle and unreflective as she is, does not fall into his error. After Henry has run away with her daughter Maria Rushworth,

> *Lady Bertram did not think deeply, but, guided by Sir Thomas, she thought justly on all important points; and she saw, therefore, in all its enormity, what had happened, and neither required herself, nor required Fanny to advise her, to think little of guilt and infamy.*[8]

To blame Jane Austen, as some commentators have done, for being '*merely conventional*' in her view of sexual morality is to fail in sympathy. Jane Austen was an unmarried clergyman's daughter in an age of religious revival and moral renewal.

Edmund is shocked that Mary Crawford looks on adultery as mere folly and does not see its wickedness, and we are invited to agree with him. '*Let other pens dwell on guilt and misery*',[9] writes Jane Austen. The phrase '*guilt and misery*' comes from Edward Gibbon's *Decline and Fall of the Roman Empire*, Chapter 15. The context gives a clue to the way we are to interpret the influence of the flippant, town-bred Crawfords who bring corruption into rural society. Gibbon writes:

> *It was the universal sentiment, both of the church and heretics, that the daemons were the authors, the patrons and the objects of idolatry. Those rebellious spirits who had been degraded from the rank of angels, and cast down into the infernal pit, were still permitted to roam upon earth, to torment the bodies and seduce the minds of sinful men ... they usurped the place and honours of the supreme deity. By the success of their malicious contrivances, they at once gratified their own vanity and revenge, and obtained the*

> *only comfort of which they were yet susceptible, the hope of involving the human species in ... their guilt and misery.*

While it would be an exaggeration to push the comparison too far, Mary and Henry fulfil much of the function in Mansfield society that Gibbon's daemons do in the world at large. Henry's great fault is vanity, which makes him try irresponsibly to make Fanny fall in love with him. The daemons roam the earth and seduce the minds of men; the Crawfords restlessly roam the country, and are associated, in their different ways, with the principle of seduction. Henry seduces a married woman; Mary tries to seduce the mind of Edmund away from his vocation as a priest. She tries to make him worship, instead, her secular values. She shows a worldly, aristocratic disdain for his seriousness, and accuses him of planning to be a *'celebrated preacher in some great society of Methodists'.*[10] Writing to Fanny, she frets at not seeing Edmund: *'There may be some old woman at Thornton Lacey to be converted.'*[11] *'Converted'* is a Methodist word and Mary uses it mockingly.

In Milton's epic poem, *Paradise Lost*, the fallen angels make war in heaven upon God. Mary Crawford's is *'a mind darkened, yet fancying itself light'.*[12] Jane Austen may have had in mind the constant dark-light antitheses in Milton's poem and recollected, in association with *'guilt and misery'*, the fallen angel whose form holds *'still her original brightness'*. Mary Crawford, like those deposed spirits who have become fallen angels, wandering daemons, is dangerous, a temptress.

Mary and Henry have charm and vivacity; they have neither religion nor good morals. Careful reading shows that Jane Austen could never have intended them to be appealing and then changed her mind while writing, as some commentators have suggested. Their selfishness is betrayed by every word the pair say. It is worth remembering that Bishop Sherlock's sermons were among Jane Austen's favourite reading. She would probably have endorsed Jane West's view of *'the blessed effects of the Sabbath in an orderly country village ... the great civiliser of the lower orders'*. Jane Austen's cousins, the Cookes, welcomed *Mansfield Park*: they liked, in particular, its picture of clerical duty.

The place of the theatricals in *Mansfield Park* has given rise to much misunderstanding. A look at the historical context clarifies much that has puzzled modern readers. We know that Jane

Austen took part in amateur theatricals as a girl, but it seems her opinions changed later in life, under the influence of the Evangelical movement. Evangelicals strongly disapproved of gambling, Sunday travelling and home acting; some even disapproved of dancing.

Edmund says '*private theatricals are open to some objections*'.[13] The objections Edmund entertains, within the action of the novel, are probably those expressed by Gisborne: private theatricals are '... *almost certain to prove ... injurious to the female performers ... to destroy diffidence, by the unrestrained familiarity with persons of the other sex, which inevitably results*'. The narrative also makes the point that it is arguably heartless for the young people to be amusing themselves in such a way while their father is on a perilous journey. They also waste a great deal of money on labour and materials at a time of financial anxiety.

The crucial point, though, is that the '*unrestrained familiarity*' between Henry and Maria (who is engaged, through her own wilfulness, to a man she does not love) leads to their later flight and disgrace. Maria and Henry Crawford play the parts of mother (Agatha) and son (Frederick), which allows them fond embraces. Fanny is embarrassed that they choose to rehearse these affectionate and demonstrative scenes with such enthusiasm and so often. As she and Edmund recognize, the play puts Maria, who is in love with Henry, in a tense and tempting situation. Mary Crawford plays Amelia, Frederick's half-sister. Her part requires her to make bold advances to her tutor, the clergyman Anhalt, played by Edmund. Mary finds this potentially distressing, since she is in love with Edmund; she asks Fanny to help her rehearse, which causes Fanny pain, since she too loves Edmund. Edmund, who does not originally intend to act, allows himself to be drawn in to save Mary the embarrassment of acting with a stranger. The episode of the theatricals is used with great subtlety to weave the web of the characters' emotions.

Embarrassment and tension are generated, along with a dangerous irritability, in the Mansfield circle: jealousies are rife, both about the allocation of parts and over emotional relationships. Competition for the part of Agatha, with its affectionate relationship to Frederick (Henry Crawford), causes ill-feeling between Maria and Julia. Maria's triumph in getting the part, however, is short-lived, since her hopes that Henry will declare his love for her, so she can marry him instead of her boring fiancé, come to nothing. Fanny is jealous of Edmund's absorption in his part and in Mary. As Edmund says later, the time of the play was a time of general folly.

The text of *Lovers' Vows* is appended to the Oxford edition of *Mansfield Park*. It does not strike the modern reader as improper; it makes very dull reading. Yet Edmund considers it '*exceedingly unfit for private representation*'. Maria argues that it will be all right '*with a very few omissions*'. Lady Bertram says: '*Do not act anything improper, my dear, Sir Thomas would not like it.*'[14] And when Sir Thomas comes home, he does not like it.

The story of *Lovers' Vows* is as follows: Frederick, a soldier, finds his mother, Agatha, in poverty. She has been seduced and abandoned by Baron Wildenhaim. Frederick, learning the truth, goes out to beg so he can support her. He accidentally meets his father and tries to rob him. Frederick is arrested and finds out from his half-sister, Amelia, that he has threatened his own father. Amelia is under pressure to marry the foolish Count Cassell, although she is in love with her tutor, the clergyman Anhalt. Cassell is a heartless womanizer and shameless about admitting it. Anhalt persuades the Baron to listen to Frederick's excuses. Frederick makes a plea to the Baron about the hardships of being an illegitimate son.

> '*After five years' absence from my mother, I returned this very day and found her dying in the streets for want,*' says Frederick, '*...In this house did you rob my mother of her honour; and in this house I am a sacrifice for the crime ... when you turn your head from my extended corse, you will behold my weeping mother....*'

Anhalt effects a reconciliation between the Baron, who is anxious to expiate, and Agatha: they get married. Frederick is accepted as their son. The reformed Baron also allows his daughter to marry for love.

Fanny objects to the characters of Agatha and Amelia as '*totally improper for home representation—the situation of one and the language of the other, so unfit to be expressed by any woman of modesty*'.[15]

The objection to Agatha is explained by Jane West: she is a woman of '*lost character*'—an unmarried mother. The objection to Amelia is that she makes bold love to her tutor, the clergyman Anhalt. She introduces the subject of marriage and he makes a long speech beginning, '*When two sympathetic hearts meet in the marriage state, matrimony may be called a happy life ...*' Amelia tells him boldly, '*I am in love*' and begs him to teach her love: '*teach it me as you taught me geography, languages, and other important things*'. By twisting his words in reply, she actually proposes marriage to him. For a woman to propose to a man was a serious breach of decorum.

Julia considers the part of Amelia '*disgusting....I quite detest her. An odious, little, pert, unnatural, impudent girl.*'[16]

William Cobbett wrote in 1801:

> *Amelia, notwithstanding the pains which Mrs Inchbald, the adaptor ... has taken to polish her, still remains coarse, forward and disgusting, and, we trust, will never be imitated by the British fair.*

The play was both popular and notorious. Jane Austen wrote assuming that readers would know both the plot and the play's bad reputation. While she was living in Bath, there were six performances of *Lovers' Vows* at the Theatre Royal, and it was often performed on the London stage. It was also generally recognized as being morally and politically subversive. Edmund's advice is to change the play.

It was translated from the German and although German influence on the English stage reached its peak at the turn of the century, German plays were objected to because good rarely triumphed over evil. Mrs Trimmer, in *The Guardian of Education* (1802) wrote of '*German poison*'; '*a torrent of infidelity*'. Jane West attacked German writers for their '*infidelity and scepticism*' and the '*monstrous extravagancies of German morality*'. She complains of '*pseudo-sentimental moralists...*' who '*adorn sin in such soft colours*'. The poet Wordsworth (1770–1850) wrote of '*sickly and stupid German tragedies*'. The critic William Hazlitt, his contemporary, enjoyed them, but admitted that '*their moral is immorality*'. He justified his preference by arguing that the plays were topical: they embodied '*...the extreme opinions which are floating in our time*'. Extreme opinions were what the conservative and religious, with the example of the French Revolution behind them, were afraid of.

Lovers' Vows was considered immoral because its message was that man was naturally good (cf. Rousseau); social equality was desirable; instinct was a better guide to behaviour than morality. It showed the upper classes as depraved, the lower classes as worthy and virtuous. This was politically explosive.

There is an anticipation in the casting of Maria as Agatha in that both are '*women of lost character*' who break the moral code. Taking the part puts Maria in the way of the temptation to which she eventually succumbs when she becomes Henry's mistress. *Lovers' Vows* fulfils Gisborne's worst fears in that acting in it proves injurious to at least one female performer through unrestrained familiarity with a person of the opposite sex. Agatha in the play is allowed to resume her place in society, by marrying her seducer. Maria is banished to a sort of house arrest with Mrs Norris.

Lovers' Vows was suspect as an expression of sexual laxity (Cobbett explained that no fallen woman should come to a happy ending on stage), radicalism, subversion and even atheism. As Tories like Dr Johnson and Jane Austen saw it, society was threatened by political and moral revolt. They preferred tradition, conservation and unimproved estates. It was the Whigs who built houses in the Palladian style as a political statement, an endorsement of Roman (and by implication republican) values.[17]

There is no doubt that Jane Austen considered the play as objectionable as Edmund and Fanny do. It was introduced into Mansfield by the Hon. John Yates, a foolish sprig of aristocracy for whom the respectable Sir Thomas feels only contempt. The dangerous opinions put forward in such works as *Lovers' Vows* were flirted with by the Whig aristocrats. Jane Austen saw it as the duty of the Tory gentry to resist such people and their corrupting influences. Religious and political stability, which she valued profoundly, could in her view only be maintained by responsible moral leadership from the landowning and professional classes, whose private lives had to be as impeccable as their public ones. As we have seen, she demands of her characters more than '*good breeding*': those she admires have good hearts. In this, she was in tune with an inherited strand of moral teaching. She accepted, with others in her age, that right thinking and right feeling must be firmly based on religious principle.

NOTE: The full text of the play *Lovers' Vows* should be consulted in the Oxford edition of *Mansfield Park*.
[1] Jane Austen *Mansfield Park* pp. 247–8   [2] *ibid*. p. 340   [3] *ibid*. p. 87   [4] *ibid*. p. 92   [5] *ibid*. p. 440   [6] *ibid*. p. 41   [7] *ibid*. p. 296   [8] *ibid*. p. 449   [9] *ibid*. p. 461   [10] *ibid*. p. 458   [11] *ibid*. p. 394   [12] *ibid*. p. 367   [13] *ibid*. p. 125   [14] *ibid*. p. 140   [15] *ibid*. p. 137   [16] *ibid*. p. 136   [17] I am grateful for this information to Miss Janet Ball of Lucy Cavendish College, Cambridge

Bibliography

BIOGRAPHICAL

JENKINS, ELIZABETH *Jane Austen* (Gollancz, 1938)   The standard biography

VIPONT, ELFRIDA *A little bit of ivory: A life of Jane Austen* (Hamish Hamilton, 1977)   A readable outline

LETTERS

AUSTEN, JANE *Letters, 1796–1817* Selected and edited by R. W. Chapman ('World's Classics' series O.U.P., 1955)   Dr Chapman was the editor of the complete two-volume edition of the letters which may be consulted in public libraries. It has recently been reprinted.

WALPOLE, H. *Letters* Selected and edited by C. B. Lucas (Simpkin, Marshall, Hamilton, Kent & Co. Ltd)

CRITICAL AND BACKGROUND STUDIES

There is an enormous volume of writing about Jane Austen. I select here a few books which I have found useful. Readers should explore libraries and make their own discoveries.

HARDING, D. W. 'Regulated hatred' Reprinted in *Jane Austen,* edited by Ian Watt ('Twentieth Century Views' series, Prentice-Hall, 1963)   This short essay marks a turning point in Jane Austen criticism. Instead of a bland reflector of her society, she is increasingly seen now as an analytical critic of it.

KAYE-SMITH, SHEILA AND STERN, G. B. *Talking of Jane Austen* (Cassell, 1943) This book, with its sequel, *More talk of Jane Austen,* is unfashionable because its tone is cosy and chatty. However, it is a helpful introduction to beginners, because although the authors are sometimes superficial, they direct the reader to the fine detail of Jane Austen's wit.

LEAVIS, Q. D. 'Introduction to *Mansfield Park*' Reprinted in *Jane Austen: Sense and Sensibility, Pride and Prejudice and*

Mansfield Park Critical essays edited by B. C. Southam (Macmillan 'Casebook' series, 1976)

LODGE, D. 'The vocabulary of *Mansfield Park*' An essay included in his book *The language of fiction* (Routledge and Kegan Paul, 1966) Highly recommended.

MUDRICK, M. *Irony as defense and discovery* (Princeton U.P., 1962) Professor Mudrick's book is uneven. His challenging interpretations have been considered wilful and perverse by many Jane Austen enthusiasts, but he probes deeply. His account of *Sense and Sensibility*, in particular, cannot be ignored.

SOUTHAM, B. C. *Jane Austen* ('Writers and their work' series, Longman for the British Council, 1976) I am indebted to Mr Southam's sociological investigations and shrewd criticism.

TANNER, T. Introductions to the Penguin editions of *Sense and Sensibility*, *Pride and Prejudice* and *Mansfield Park*

WRIGHT, A. *Jane Austen's novels: A study in structure* (Chatto and Windus, 1953) A helpful all round study

MORE SPECIALIZED STUDIES

BUTLER, MARILYN *Jane Austen and the War of Ideas* (O.U.P., 1975) Explains the controversies of the eighteenth century and Jane Austen's relation to them.

DUCKWORTH, A. M. *The improvement of the estate: A study of Jane Austen's novels* (Johns Hopkins U.P., 1971) Scrupulous, thoughtful and illuminating.

PHILLIPPS, K. C. *Jane Austen's English* (Andre Deutsch, 1970) Teases out the finer shades of meaning. Essential for all advanced students.

TOLER, K. *Jane Austen's art of allusion* (Nebraska, 1968) Original and relevant study of Jane Austen's literary references, which often turn out to be crucial for interpretation.

WORKS CONTEMPORARY WITH JANE AUSTEN

MALTHUS, T. *An essay on the principle of population* (First published 1798, Pelican classics, 1970)

WHITE, G. *The natural history of Selborne* (First published 1789, 'World's Classics' series, O.U.P.)

WOLLSTONECRAFT, MARY *A vindication of the rights of woman* (First published 1792, Penguin, 1975) Also recommended is Claire Tomalin's prizewinning biography *The life and death of Mary Wollstonecraft* (Weidenfeld & Nicolson, 1974)

WOODFORDE, J. Passages from the five volumes of the *Diary of a Country Parson 1758–1802* Selected and edited by John Beresford (O.U.P., 1935)

YOUNG, A. *Autobiography with selections from his correspondence* Edited by M. Betham Edwards First published 1898

FURTHER READING

ARMSTRONG, A. *Church of England, the Methodists and Society 1700–1850* (London U.P., 1973)

BOVILL, E. W. *English country life 1770–1830* (O.U.P., 1962)

BRANDER, M. *The Georgian gentleman* (Saxon House, 1973)

BROWN, F. K. *Fathers of the Victorians* (Cambridge U.P., 1961)

JAEGER, MURIEL *Before Victoria* (Chatto and Windus, 1956)

MARSHALL, DOROTHY *English people in the eighteenth century* (Longmans, 1956)

TINDAL HART, A. *The curate's lot* (John Baker, 1970)

WILLIAMS, E. N. *Life in Georgian England* (Batsford, 1962)

Appendix

CUSTOMS AT THE DANCE

(Letter to the *Sunday Times*, 4th January 1948. See Chapter 8.)

Sir,—Brigadier Bliss asks why in *Pride and Prejudice* the first dance is called the first 'two' and the second dance the second 'two'. The reason is that Jane Austen was writing in the days of the minuet, and acceptance of a dance still carried with it two dances, or the twice going up and down in a minuet. This custom seems to have fallen out of use with the introduction of the less formal and more energetic dances, e.g. the waltz in 1813 and the polka in 1844.

... In *Evelina*, published in 1778, it is clear that the custom of dancing with the same partner throughout the evening was still in vogue, and it was this constraint that made Evelina guilty of a breach of manners when she refused a more undesirable partner and waited until the more engaging Lord Orville asked for her hand. Such was not the case in *Pride and Prejudice*, written only 20 years later, and Mrs Bennett could boast that Jane was the only lady with whom Mr Bingley danced a second 'two'.

It may reasonably be conjectured that this change took place in the last quarter of the eighteenth century, and this does not contradict Mrs Delaney, who died in 1773 and whose letters were earlier. 'Ladies to draw for places' means probably places in the first minuet. Usually the most distinguished lady led the dance from the top of the room, with the remainder following, sometimes in precedence. This might be invidious, and at a public dance might be avoided by a draw.

Michael Chavasse, Rochester

Index